The North is a publication of

the poetry business

The magazine is published twice a year.
Edited by Ann Sansom and Peter Sansom. Reviews Editor: Holly Hopkins

Copyright © 2024 The Contributors
All Rights Reserved
ISSN 0269-9885
ISBN 978-1-914914-65-2

Designed & typeset by Utter Design utter.co.uk.
Cover image: Peasants Celebrating Twelfth Night by David Teniers the Younger.
Printed by Page Bros.

No part of this publication may be reproduced without the consent of the publishers.

We are currently only considering work submitted online (not by post). Please go to www.poetrybusiness.co.uk/about/submissions/ for more details.

We are grateful for the financial assistance of Arts Council England.

Distributed by BookSource, 50 Cambuslang Road, Cambuslang Investment Park, Glasgow G32 8NB.

Advertising rates on request.

Subscribe to The North

Current rate is £22 per annum or £44 for two years (digital version £16/£22), single copies £12 (digital version £9) (overseas print subscription £28 per annum or £56 for two years, single copies £14).

Subscription address:
The Poetry Business,
Campo House, 54 Campo Lane
Sheffield S1 2EG tel 0114 4384074.
www.poetrybusiness.co.uk/product-category/the-north/subscriptions/

Correspondence address:
email: office@poetrybusiness.co.uk

Please make cheques etc. payable to The Poetry Business

www.poetrybusiness.co.uk

N70 POETRY

110 POEMS BY 64 POETS

Anastasia Taylor-Lind
Anthony Wilson
Emily Wills
Rebecca Cullen
Graham Mort
Christine Webb
Rachael Brown
Matthew Paul
Emma Lara Jones
Simon Armitage
Mary Chuck
Jay Whittaker
Pascale Petit
James Caruth
Alicia Stubbersfield
Ian Dudley
Alexandra Corrin-Tachibana
Tom Sastry
Helen Mort
Maria Taylor
Julian Turner
Paul Stephenson
Fiona Larkin
Ruth Sharman
Duncan Chambers
Sarah Mnatzaganian
Dzifa Benson
Lou Neuberger
Claudine Toutoungi
Jonathan Edwards

Ben Bransfield
Orlagh O'Farrell
D A Prince
Kathryn Bevis
Jane Kite
Kate Bass
Sue Norton
Michael Schmidt
Carrie Etter
Kathy Pimlott
Mary Ford Neal
Paul Henry
Laura Strickland
Ian McMillan
Pam Thompson
Helen Bowell
Prerani Kumar
Eva Lewis
Laura Potts
Ruth Yates
Caleb Leow
Freya Bantiff
Doreen Gurrey
Laurie Bolger
Mary Allen
Clementine Burnley
Michael Greavy
Lydia Harris
Ramona Herdman
Lauren O'Donovan

Ali Lewis
Alan Payne
Shash Trevett
Jane Routh

For A Full List Of Poems Please See Back Pages

N70 PROSE

FEATURES

Blind Criticism 57
Shash Trevett and **Mark Pajak**

Poets I Go Back To 84
Holly Hopkins and **Abigail Parry**

Featured Title 88
Ali Lewis, Absence, CHEERIO Publishing

PUBLICATIONS

New Poets Prize 2023 Winners 66

International Book & Pamphlet Competition Winners 2023 72

Book & Pamphlet Competition Highly Commended Poets 76

Various Poets
Coal: An anthology for the 40th anniversary of the Miners' Strike 70

Alan Payne
Mahogany Eve 90

Shash Trevett
The Naming of Names 94

Jane Routh
The Luck 98

REVIEWS

Angela Cleland 103
on Sarala Estruch, Amy Acre, Isabel Galleymore

Belinda Cooke 106
on Peter Sirr, Harry Clifton

Ian McMillan 110
on Guillaume Apollinaire translated by Martin Sorrell, Charlotte Gann, Blake Morrison, Gill Shaw, Emily Oldfield, Elvire Roberts, Jan Norton

Jonathan Davidson 113
on Robert Selby, Helen Tookey, Kathryn Simmonds. David Clarke

Edmund Prestwich 116
on Kit Fan, Hasan Alizadeh translated and introduced by Kayvan Tahmasebian and Rebecca Ruth Gould

James Caruth 119
on Mark Roper, Jane Clarke, Gillian Clarke

Suzanne Conway 122
on Fiona Benson, John Wedgwood Clarke, Rosie Jackson

Theophilus Kwek 126
on Momtaza Mehri, Khairani Barokka, Zaffar Kunial

EDITORIAL

Welcome to *The North 70*, an aria on hope, as the second poem in has it, what a wonderful poem (and issue) it is, hope you agree. A world within a world, where hopefulness may be 'a blank sheet acting / as a canvas for anything that can be written or drawn'. Though even so, all too often it is a world that 'cries out in pain'. Which is why it seemed necessary to put first that harrowing piece by an outstanding poet who is also a news photographer – a remarkable, hurt poem that is obliged to detail war at first hand. The third poem in this issue is personal in another way and is literally about remembering – the central metaphor a memory of a mnemonic, in fact. A poem which manages to bring before us a person and a friendship, and in which by 'trying to remember', it invokes Caroline, a friend of the poet's from medical school, 'always top in anatomy, and so nice about it, you couldn't not like her. 'Sweet Caroline,' the poem wittily and tenderly says, 'I'd forgotten the words to the tune of you.'

Or perhaps you don't read magazines from page one on, but just dip in and out. Or maybe you turn first to familiar names, which in this issue might be among others Simon Armitage or Graham Mort, Helen Mort or Pascale Petit, all as it happens represented by quite differently brilliant poems. We hope there are many differently brilliant poems in this issue also by poets that are new to you.

Open the magazine anywhere, anyway, and it's likely to be a really remarkable poem, and incidentally one that avoids drawing attention to its writer, all the better to do what it does, and to say what it says; a poem in its own right, and even if an expression of its author, quite separate to them. And if by chance you open the magazine and don't find a poem like this, then without doubt you have turned to some prose. Which reminds us that, as with every issue, we can't believe our luck in being able to commission such a wide-ranging, entertaining and insightful set of features and reviews. Which reminds us that from this issue we are assisted by Holly Hopkins, who has taken over from Suzannah Evans as main reviews editor as well as lead editor for our New Poets List. Our latest new(er) poets are also outstanding, as you will see in these pages: our New Poets Prize winners as well as the five poets in our latest NP anthology, *Five*. In this issue we're delighted too to feature the winners and runners-up in the 2023/2024 International Book & Pamphlet Competition. Courtesy of that year's judge, Hannah Lowe. (Congratulations all and thank you Hannah for choosing so well!)

But to return to the other half (the larger half) of the magazine, the poems. As editors we may not be avowed sensation seekers, but it's fair to say we're not fans of the dull but worthy. And we're fortunate in having so many excellent and diverting and genuine poems to choose from. For this latest issue (as usual) we had well over a thousand submissions. So it's worth pointing out that of course we were obliged to overlook a lot of excellent poems. If yours were in among, please do send more in due course. And meanwhile also look at the magazine's on-line off-shoot, *East of The North*. This very full space on our website presents new poems, photos and audio, and trails new articles and interviews as well as blogs, poems and other material from The Poetry Business's digital poets in residence.

'An Aria on Hope' (by Anthony Wilson), where this editorial began, is a poem in memory of (and borrows something of the style of) John Ash (1948-2019), a poet who was important to many people, including us. More recently – very recently, so that we still can't quite believe it – we heard of the deaths of Yvonne Green and Geoff Hattersley. Their writing is very different from each other's and indeed from any other poet's and, as many of you will know, outstanding. Geoff's first book in over a decade, *Instead of an Alibi*, was published in 2023 by Broken Sleep. Also last year, Hendon Press brought out Yvonne's translations of the Soviet-Ukranian poet, Semyon Lipkin. Some of their work and details of other publications appears on our website.

Please go to www.poetrybusiness.co.uk for details of all our publications and our latest programme of guest-tutored online workshops, as well as to check out *East of The North*, for more poems and features, including one on favourite poems from the first 70 issues, and how you might vote for your own favourite *North* poems. From which incidentally we hope next year to compile an anthology. Watch this space or somewhere close by. Meanwhile, good reading – and spread the word would you about this fabulous as always 70th issue.

ANASTASIA TAYLOR-LIND

All I have is a list of things

Empty windows in Hostomel wave as I walk by,
the bright fabrics of each living room
billowing like handkerchiefs.

Apartment facades smashed open, homes like dolls houses –
kitchen, cabinets, bathroom, bath, bookcase full of books.
Emergency workers dig for bodies in the debris.

A man in uniform abseils down an open wall with a body tied into rope,
the dead man splits the body-bag and falls three storeys
while his mother watches.

KIDS written on printer paper and taped to windshields.
Along the highway, car after car stopped, shot out –
every driver's door flung open.

Abandoned Russian positions littered with half-filled bottles of piss.
Plastic bottle necks all touched by the soft tips of soldier's dicks
while they kept watch at these windows.

At night somewhere in the city, outgoing – Gu-gum, gu-gum, gu-gum,
distant as thunder through the double glazing. 20 kilometers away
someone is suffering under this.

ANTHONY WILSON

Aria on Hope
i.m. John Ash

Hopefulness is a blank sheet acting
as a canvas for anything that can be written
or drawn. Darkness is a metaphor
luring you into a cave of unknowing.
The world cries out in pain and you with it,
remembering your mother. The watch
you wear on your wrist, how is that a cloud?
Stories from childhood burn themselves
onto your midnight retina as you lie sweating.
The acorn scatters its seed a hundred years
from now and in this way becomes a poem.
Art, that longed-for crisis of the soul,
soothes but does not bathe. In any case,
whether you paid for the experience
or came by it for free, it becomes important
to record the emotion, rinsed of feeling,
and hail the lonely piper standing vigil
at the ruined palisades and catafalques
seeing them for what they were, emblems
of a way of life long since departed.

EMILY WILLS

Mnemonic

Trying to remember, I invoke Caroline,
always top in anatomy, and so nice about it
you couldn't not like her. Caroline, I envied
the sleek of your hair, grace of your bones,
even your backstory, a mother died young
from a lymphoma curable by the time we met,
a stepmother you never mentioned. Sweet Caroline,
I'd forgotten the words to the tune of you,
how you scried your skin for lumps and bruises,
malignant portents, swollen glands.

You'd slipped from my mind, ditto the bones of the wrist,
innervation of the gut, the order of structures
lateral to medial towards the navel. But now, as I peer
into the dissection of the past, back it comes
in a reek of formalin – the nerves, the sweats,
those frantic incantations to short-term memory –

Nerve, Artery, Vein, Empty space, Lymphatic.

Famous

My father wrote to Laurie Lee, having recognised
in *Cider with Rosie*, his mother's distant cousin Charlie
sprawled in a buttercup field in Slad

dubiously related but still part of the lineage
renowned even beyond the hinterlands of Stroud
for Stone's Self Raising Flour.

I still have the reply, in pencil, with its 3p stamp
appreciating *your interesting letter* but no,
it was a different Charlie, whose father owned a bootshop

where the son should have been, that sultry afternoon
heeling and soling in a rubbery fume
on the other side of town from the bakery

in which my father's Charlie, relatively unclear,
may actually have stood, dreaming of long grass
trying to cool his pastry hands.

The bootshop's still there, wrote Laurie in '73
but the son left years ago, likewise my grandmother,
who abandoned self-raising to marry a Methodist Minister

thereby securing my possession of this eminent signature –
I salute the Stone side of your family
whose fame I knew, sincerely yours

REBECCA CULLEN

Oh Twenties
After Kenneth Koch

Years of my slim-hipped shimmy, zip of thigh-high boots,
short skirts, long curls. The glory of you, bright-eyed,
capable of every possibility imaginable and some you can't.
Because come to think of it you had no plan, fell in
with ways to earn a living that made people gasp and say
'Wow! Twenties! You've got it made, you've got it all worked out!'
Walking-strutting-dancing with a permanently-appended
cigarette, you were the star in your own film noir,
knocking on the doors of secret restaurants at 2 am
while men in sharp suits played poker in the back room.

Twenties, when I think about you now, my chest
is tight because I should have held you to myself
instead of losing you and not keeping in touch.
I was the same with my teens; should have known better.
Instead I've got the Fifties here to stay and Christ,
do they go on. Not like you, Twenties, quick of tongue
and sharp as well, sometimes told 'You're so sharp
you'll cut yourself' and ah, my two zero friends,
you cut through mud and tears and frenemies;
we both know who we're talking about.

Do you remember when you gave me lychees
and they weren't eyeballs after all? Every six months,
when I was summoned by the bank, you held my hand.
It's true you paid bills late but always had a fiver
for the pub. Twenties, you were loyal but fleeting;
I was wrong to think you'd go on forever. You sang
and cried and there was nothing in-between.
You taught me loneliness. You brought me love.
You are my favourite, Twenties, always ready
for a night out. Ready now. I know you're up for it.

Meanwhile they're demolishing the Broadmarsh Centre

The department stores are being picked apart;
steel rods stick out, each ceiling in cross-section
like a concrete Lion Bar.

From the tram, it's a settlement re-emerging
after a drought; an excavation of empty boxes
once filled with fridges, menswear, clocks.

I bought two precious sofas there, a negligee.
I loved the wooden cricket climbing frame,
the children's shoe shop with the spinning chimp.

Where are all the floor staff now? Where
have they gone? Do they muster in the new
multi-storey, wishing they could come home?

Broad Marsh. First you were houses.
Then you housed the second-best shops.
We built you up to tear you down.

GRAHAM MORT

Triton

I thought I dreamed you slept on a door
painted ocean green   a beautiful man

pulled from the waves   a triton   a sea
satyr spewing founts of jewelled water.

I dreamt of our room in that house with
the North Sea in it   pine boards creaking

as we took to bed   lay in its sepulchral
sheets   making small talk or love as the

hours shrank   then widened the moon's
trail across a dazzling meniscus   the

phosphorescence of herring shoals   its
sheen of salt   nacre of finned creatures

sheathed in slime. We slept through that
fabled hour before the dawn   darker

by far   waking at noon   completed by the
night   rounded as sea-fruit   re-born

exotic   full of the spice of a tide's gravity
glinting among sea-glass and scented

bladder-wrack   wet pebbles shot with ore.
Now are autumn gales   equinoctial days

where memory staggers in the shallows
before sleep. I remember those un-

caulked boards calling out as we rose to
make coffee   smoke of the kipper house

a white haar   a fine sea-fret. I see you
stepping from my thoughts   floundering

from a storm's lees   that waning   waxing
waning moon   to greet me   to breathe air

to lie on a green door that keeps opening

CHRISTINE WEBB

Oyster Catcher Dawn

We hear an oyster catcher before dawn
waking us to this present tense allowing

our memory of chiaroscuro hills the first
rain in weeks streaking dusted glass shapes

of the room remembering themselves
a luminous watch the outline of a book

a glass of water its bubbles of breathable
air a blister pack of pills the door prised

open the glow of a nightlight entering my
thoughts that did handstands all night

forming and pulling apart as if nothing
in my body could release them then that

call again spiralling over the village and its
sleepers disclosing a silver liquidity until

a car engine fires a neighbour goes to work
leaving me with your outline against the

sheets thinking *I know you if nothing else* so
without ever speaking reaching for your

shoulder then thinking *I never did or could*
the rain harder the thoughts never now but

then so recollected daylight reaching us as
breeze dents curtains the call of that mono-

chrome bird repeating from its scarlet bill
its carmine legs trailing spilling day into what

has been or is or will be again the night.

Gift

The boy was fourteen. Josh. Dark hair, good hands.
He came with his mother, brought a tape measure,
took shots from several angles – *to show Dad.*
It'll fit on the wall against the stairs, won't it?
He pulled out the stool, touched his fingers to the keys
and everything about him changed – his spine,
set of his shoulders, the way his head
became attentive. He started to play.

No one had touched the piano in months. Its pitch
wavered, but its many singing voices
awoke, and filled the room with possibility.
When he stopped playing, we were all silent
until he swung round, looked at his mother and me.

I said I didn't want paying. It was a gift.

RACHAEL BROWN

Sunk Cost Fallacy

try harder   wind through leaves is not your mother
shaking plastic bags   this is you running
hey washing line! hey dreamcatcher!
not sure what to do with all the voices
you are snagging your mother says
this hedgerow disappeared
so it's going   something about
no money no money no money
take five   in Aldi unable to breathe
for cucumbers whose condoms you are not
decrying   decision it's cost and reward
here's the therapist she wants to know
if there's sufficient air down your t-shirt
for inflation   this is you   billowing
with things you are not currently
back on the road it's a warm November
hey bicep emoji! hey Fitbit! hey Lycra!
at this stage Alexa says electrolytes matter
take a run through your unfinished
business   self-five at the clock
with your face on greenbelt
tightens don't ask
when fence posts creep
into clover   far out a father
and daughter up to their waists in
cow parsley guess whose dining room
they are standing in whose perfect
cheese plants   the road is a fake
barricaded pretends   it could be
Spain   it could be kerbside flogging
glowsticks for rent the inevitable
snapping 9pm Whatsapp Plastic

in Breast Milk later in bed here's
the person you love saying things
are quite far gone now hands
and hands are holding shut
drawers inside which are
carefully bubblewrapped
future names

Against all advice

John remembers a conversation he once had
and is back on a pleasant street.

This time the trees have been carefully
worded, and he waits patiently at red lights.

God bless John the Tourist; he admires expensive sticks,
the diligence of street sweepers keeping the blank street clean.

And God bless John the Topiarist; he clips park shrubs
in his best suit, pockets the offcuts.

The sky is light polluted and so unavailable,
but God bless John the Empiricist who knows umbrellas are practical.

He draws one out in front of him and, in doing so,
has done it now. The trees

are spitting tin tacks, umbrellas
hurtle on broken wings and everything and John

is a shrinking July night   one black cab
crawling to the end of its line as the road comes
        rolling behind like a carpet
                        the very sky
unpeels itself and the last house standing dims its lights
on portraits
        downstairs smiling

MATTHEW PAUL

Invigilator Slater

I fail the first O-level Physics paper
    with over an hour to spare.

Ball-bearings rain bashes the corrugated-iron
    roof of the Nissen-hut gym.

I take *Zen and the Art of Motorcycle Maintenance*
    from my pocket, and Mr Slater,

our English teacher, baby-giraffes his corduroy-
    jacketed six-feet-eight between

Gorgeous-George-the-caretaker's neat lines of desks
    to whisper, 'Betcha don't finish it.'

EMMA LARA JONES

Outside the hospital

There's an algae-thick pond near the car park
close to the cancer wellness centre.
A few wooden benches by a gravel path

where patients sit and watch the water.
Drowning hazard! warns a sign
in the flaking font of an ancient sutra.

Here's a frail woman with an IV line
a relative alone with his cigarette
a mother duck, her ducklings splash behind

mask-eyed like cartoon bandits.
Small beaks flutter the pond's surface
tipping their heads to savour each sip.

While pairs of swans drift past unhurried
in the white coats of pathologists.

God bless urban architects

My joy begins with oblong wheels
painted on the cycle path
the kind slope of the bus shelter roof
the cat's cradle of iron bars
that protect the park.
And who painted that metal roof
the spruce green of a Christmas tree
or gave the school its wide
rainbow-rimmed eyes?
Even the red of the dog waste bin
could suggest the thrill of a posted letter.
Each manhole cover adorned with
a careful grid of tesserae.

SIMON ARMITAGE

The Holy Land

What were you thinking, kid,
the moon egging you on,
the west wind whispering
give it some knuckle,
give it some edge.
There you go, cock of the north
with your rainwater face-paint
and home-cut hair,
riding your quad bike bronco
across the fields
with a brainless power tool
under a drover's coat.

What boozy sap
or red diesel
pulsed through your jugular, lad,
scaling the tumbledown wall
and planting the fuck-them-all flag,
feeling the tight grain
crumble like bread
as the chainsaw yawned
then breezed through hundreds of years
of weather and kings and wars
and blah blah blah.

Then the green horizon
crashed through the toppled sky,
didn't it, boy,
and noiseless swat teams
of seed propellers suddenly swarmed
in the void, midnight's radar
showing a blank screen
till the twin white discs
of lopped trunk and raw stump
loomed in the night.

There's a gap now in the Gap
where your face fits,
where your mugshot sits.
A candlelit vigil
smoulders and fumes
between hills
as the sun sets.
And they'll make a nice bench
from the planed wood
or whittle an angel
or turn some knot or burr
into burnished treen.

But I'm not here
to nail teenage flesh
to a timber cross,
not here to witness you
walking the plank, son,
or watch the lynch mob
lasso a branch
with a hangman's noose.
That sycamore saint had become
a movie extra
or mindfulness poster
or Instagram pose – truth is
one tree can't breathe
for the whole world – truth is
I was you once, bud,
hacking at beech bark,
slashing at ancient oaks.

The carpenter's art
begins with a death;
now build a forest,
now plant a house,
now carve a leaf.

MARY CHUCK

A Flurry of Feathers

Blue-black roof tiles against a blue-black sky
light changing with the angles.
Easy-peeler brick chimneys catch the morning sun.
The spire of St Elphin's just visible in winter
too far to hear the bells.
Disembodied, the red light at the top
of a ship's mast passes along the Ship Canal;
sometimes a foghorn, a warning to the swing bridge.
Squirrel in the lilac and onto the silver birch.
Sparrows, blue tits and goldfinches on the bird-feeder.
And only once a sparrow hawk. She stayed for
nearly half an hour, ripping and tearing at her prey.

Grandson visiting

Over the road and over the stream
the fields run uphill to the railway line
curving its way below the horizon
to the station.

I can walk up the hill to meet his train.
I'll see him coming round the curve.
He'll wave his red knitted cap
as he always waves.

Look there, his red cap waving.
He'll get off the train and run down the path
through the field, through the long grass
to save my legs.

I can see his red cap over the wall.
I'll walk a bit further, he'll be surprised
how far I've come. *You shouldn't have
walked so far*, he'll say.

I've missed him somewhere. Maybe he ran
right past over the wall through the long grass.
Maybe he went to see some-one else.
Maybe he'll come on the next train.

JAY WHITTAKER

Letter to My Younger Self

If I could come back and walk with you again, it
wouldn't be the great escape walks, the journeys
to far-away places to shut out the everyday 'stuff'
not the Annapurna Circuit, the Machu Picchu trail
the ascent of Kilimanjaro.

If I came back I wouldn't need the hiking boots
the walking poles, the water-proof cagoules and
over-trousers, nor even the black umbrella you
carried in the High Pyrenees when it was almost
too hot to move.

No – you / I, we'd drive out to the coast, park by
the statue of Collingwood and walk out along the
pier at the mouth of the Tyne, waves pounding
wind blowing hard enough that we'd have to hold
onto the small children.

That's the walk I'd like to do again.

An office pedestal unit completes its annual appraisal

This year I maintained my useful position
rolled tidily under a desk. My top drawer holds
Post-Its printed with logos from long-ago conferences,
BIC Biros, three staplers, two staple removers, no staples.
I am careful to treat all stationery equally,
no matter its type or how obtained.

My second drawer is a welcoming environment
for precious spoons and mugs, porridge sachets,
tissues, tampons, teabags in calming flavours
that don't require milk from the shared fridge.
I am patient with the layer of crumbs
which keep building up. I do regret stress balls
(made from inferior plastic) crumble, whatever I do.

My capacious bottom drawer is designed
to hold hanging files, although it is some years
since I saw any such thing. I care for
a stack of print-outs which pre-date lockdown
until the confidential waste bags are ready.
Behind a compressed mass of scrunched-up Tesco carriers,
grubby trainers, long forgotten.

I have proved I am ready to work alongside
another pedestal unit to hold a more challenging
range of contents. What I would like to achieve
in the coming year is a more inspirational situation
under a more aspirational desk.

PASCALE PETIT

After visiting the Museum of Doors, Pézenas,

I crept down the spiral steps onto the earth
floor of my own museum of doors –
warped portals down each side of me

led to caves of electric and gas meters.
Each door was marked with the numbers
of the beast inside mathematics.

I was six, learning to count to a hundred.
Below me, Papa warned, raged a fire
where wolves would leap from flames.

Shall I call those wolves bêtes du Gévaudan?
Or shall I call them to me like a shepherdess,
stroke their long muzzles and scythe claws

that mark them as loups-garous, hyena-
mastiffs, chimeras of my nights?
Shall I train them to turn on Papa when

his face peers through the wavy window
at the top of the stairs and his double enters?
Some meter doors open onto vistas of Lozère,

its granite mountains and ravines,
while in others Papa is playing hide and seek,
tick-tock go the meters like his heartbeat.

In one cupboard the birds he shot
re-hatch from their corpses and fly to help me.
Papa's face is covered with a cloth

and there are two of him and two of me.
Other-me hovers just below the ceiling
that bulges with cables like his veins –

she's watching what he does to his daughter.
Then she glides through the sky's warp drives
where every star is a keyhole

for angels to watch and remember.
I open my doors which are trees in the wolf-wood
where a little girl plays with her doll

dressed as a boy, clothing her little father
in a wolf-mask and fur pyjamas that she keeps
taking off and putting back on. She strips him

to the bones she's drawn on his body,
and, around the bones, in permanent ink,
a museum of doll doors that she keeps knocking on

with the hand-shaped knocker of her adult hand.

The Frozen Zoo

You must collect things for reasons you don't yet understand
  —Daniel Boorstin

Go to the cellar of your childhood and stay when the light switch
    clicks off. Find your father's mini-fridge, the one he kept beside the bed
        he died on, his last birthday gift to himself, next to the crates

of vintage champagne bought for your reunion. His pet fridge
    that he pleaded with, on winter mornings when he could hardly breathe.
        It has the blue light of rime, racks of miniature glass towers.

Here are the vials he saved for you, smoking in the dark, as if
    savouring his last cigarette above the steps
        he could no longer descend, hooked as he was to oxygen.

Your father, perhaps the last human on earth, so precious
    when you first met him again after thirty-five years. Open
        the long-closed stoppers. You know what to do.

The voices that have been telling you to collect and collect will sigh
    as you get to work. They are all here – Sudan the last white rhino,
        Benjamin the thylacine, and Saaya the black leopard,

spirit of the Kabini forests, his stem cells with their tuft of fur.
    For reasons you don't yet understand, you must imagine them
        alive, strong enough to bear your weight on their backs.

Now, mount their ghosts and go back in time, your hands around
    the neck of years, and ride down the long tunnels of the cellar
        where memories are stored. Some will be too painful,

but you'll fly through them, reach your father just before he dies.
    Whatever he has done is done, the champagne takes you both
        down strata, past rows of meter cupboards, the one

with a child's mattress and the doll whose lips you sewed shut
    so she wouldn't tell. Down the catacombs you must go, through
        the crypts and wells of the under-cities, built one over another.

Here is the room where your animals sleep. Now imagine them back into being,
    imagine the old forests, trees that took eras learning to transform
        toxic air to oxygen will sprout up as you arrive. Find the test tube

where your own cells are preserved in liquid nitrogen, for this
    is how you become a child again. No man has forced himself into you,
        no doctor has to come after the one you trusted turned you inside out.

You'll find glaciers of tears and blood. As they thaw,
    they'll turn into raging brown rivers to replenish the earth.
        Now open each vial and release the captives from your frozen zoo.

PASCALE PETIT

Stag Father

Now that I've found my father
I'm an anaconda

that's swallowed a stag,
its antlers stuck in my mouth.

They'll drop off
when my stomach digests the body.

Until then, I'll writhe through the forest
with this uncomfortable mouthful.

Papa Guêpier

Only after you die do I dare open that case I always gazed at
when the minutes stung.

It emitted a low hum as if to comfort me. Only now
do I find it full of bees. I don't know how they survived.

I tell them our predator is gone as they crawl out
and climb up my arms, mass on my face.

I can smell meadows of nectar, the honey
they made from wildflowers on Mont Aigoual.

I want you to taste your beloved Cévennes. Now I'm the girl
in a bee mask, I let my swarm of wings shimmer

in waves over my cheeks, to mesmerise your ghost.
I am the bee queen now, my workers are this mask

I must wear to face Papa the bee-eater, you
who sit opposite me every day, your beak poised to feed.

JAMES CARUTH

Looking Back

Through the room's small window
a narrow path twists up the slope
breaking a line of bare trees.
The beginning of Spring
but not a bud to be seen
on the spare branches.

A man slips a dog off the leash.
It's happy to be free.
A young woman pushes a pram,
pauses to look up at a sky
suddenly bright with cold.
A woman, a pram, a man, a dog,
figures in a landscape.

And I see you walking amongst hills,
the sharp air a kind of grief.
O I wish that you had known
another Spring, warmth
slowly stirring the soil,
a little comfort for old bones.

The Blackbird

In the scriptorium of St Comgall's
he pauses in his labours
to listen as a blackbird sings
in the branches of a rowan tree.
It's not the flowing lines of ink,
the knotted illustrations
of beast and Saint robed
in azure, sanguine, sable, gilt,
that holds the attention of God.
It's a single hand laying down
each note of its song
in a thin margin of vellum.

ALICIA STUBBERSFIELD

Resilience

Abandoned fur coats on the Oxfam Vintage rail
whisper stories of their heyday.
The nights out: a young woman slipping
her arms into silk-lined sleeves,
her coat held by the man who kissed her neck
as he stroked the fur.

My aunt's white mink with white fox collar
takes centre stage – dinner in New York,
afternoon tea at the Ritz, recalling
being piled up with others upstairs at parties.

The lucky ones avoided paint splatter,
have a second chance
worn over jeans and big boots
out in all weathers. Nothing special now
but still soft, still warm, still almost alive.
It's not real is it? says a friend

In the Supermarket

Even in the frozen food aisle
I smell them. The hot husbands
who follow women holding the list.

An unprecedented summer raises
the gamey, just-off-the-pitch
just-out-of-the-gymness of them.

Don't their women notice?
Perhaps they like it, reminded
of those first careless nights,

then the mornings when they didn't
shower so his sweat stayed all day
on their own skin.

IAN DUDLEY

Sister Mary Aquinas

Aunty Katy, you hitched up black skirts
post Vatican 2, buzzed round Palmers Green
on a moped helping the sick and desperate.

You taught at the convent and recruited
(so my mother said) naïve teenage girls
from Irish villages to The Sisters of Providence.

Keeper of family stories, a Scouser
to the bone, devout – *God will find a way*,
your Muslim doctor was *A very holy man*.

At your Jubilee the priest told us that vows
to mean anything have to be difficult:
poverty, chastity, humility, especially humility,

all trials for you who loved laughter, family, beauty.
I picture you organizing heaven,
God looking on bewildered.

Stargazing in Atacama

As we turn off the highway and douse the headlamps,
the coma of the small town in the rear view mirror
is all that's left of our light. We drive until the track

forgets and we have to stop, decanting into darkness
at the edge of a field where clockwork, metal, Olmec heads
shudder and turn; distant scientists look through their eyes.

Overhead the silver river streams to earth:
Orion drunk, the haywain in a ditch, scorpion
upended – a Zodiac you can't see,

then can't not see, even upside down.
Mars rises above the cordillera;
the sky's the blue of infinitely thin milk.

Used to living obliquely on the earth, the high
interrogative moon tells us we are far from home.
Returning through the birch white trunks of telescopes,

we come to the edge of the gorge, a drop of 50 metres
onto boulders the size of SUVs. The bed looks dry
but a trickle of green and chuckling birds tell us there's enough

water to fight for. This is where 100 headless corpses were found:
the dead absolved of the desire to drink. On the unfenced precipice,
we count the deep cups bored in the rock, dry as eye sockets.
Filled with black water, their seven lenses pinpoint the Pleiades.

ALEXANDRA CORRIN-TACHIBANA

Haibun from East Lothian

Everything alters in the changing light, and each day of our New Year stay is a shapeshifting beauty. Mid-morning, fieldfare are chattering in faded orange buckthorn. And heading to the bay, on the path that's like a small holloway, a minute trio of trumpet lichen. Not far away, pristine, and springy to touch, a colony of British woodland star moss. A mosaic of landscapes: mudflats with sinking sands, moorhens on Marl Loch, and dunes bound by deep, stubborn roots, marram and sea lyme. As we reach the beach, a pair of black-tailed godwits inhabit the far end towards Gullane Point. Endlessly burying their heads in the sand. Oblivious of us, their gaping bills like tongs for turning meat. And then, in twilight, from the wooden bridge, clouds reflecting in Peffer Burn, silver and still as an upturned knife or, sometimes, the oily pink and blue of an abalone. The spiky coral cockle I carry back from Aberlady Bay, held sideways, is a pair of birds nestling their heads together. Upside down, it is rather erotic. And for a few days, in a whitewashed cottage, I do not think of your spoilt daughter, who you say *is tremendously sad*; of my teenage son striding into my bedroom to consider his abs in the light of the bay window; or of the stranger husband in the spare room.

above marram grass
quartering short-eared owls
pursued by corvids

Life is Movement
(a zuihitsu)

お元気ですか？　　　　　　　　　　気 — spirited, vital, vigorous — energy
How are you?　　　　　　　　　　flowing through the universe.

The Cribbar (*The Beast* and *The Widow Maker*) rises up to 30 feet over Newquay's reef.

In Sigüenza, with her lover on a balcony, watching crag martins chasing insects.
Swooping, swirling, playfully looping in, resting on the Castillo wall.
Returning every summer. Like a carnival.

　　　　　Ukiyo-e (浮世絵): the floating world. Cherry blossom crossing the archipelago.

Her husband's favourite album is Yamashita Tatsuro's *Big Wave*.
Since the Eighties his taste hasn't changed.

Light constantly changes, and that alters the atmosphere and beauty of things (Monet).

Watching a storm on Fistral beach. *Why can't boys marry their mummies?*

　　　　　In a Sigüenzan studio,
　　　　　a jeweller threading balls of coral, like giant rose hips.
　　　　　Imagine them bobbing over a polo neck.

Shimizu Minato Matsuri — a port festival.
- taeko drummers in *mawashi*
- *takoyaki* octopus balls
- shaved flavoured ice
- an outside person, joining the dance

Those who do not move, do not notice their chains (Rosa Luxembourg).

Rajio taiso, morning drill:
children and teachers in a sun-bleached yard
bending and stretching to archaic piano music
beside a pond with greedy carp
　　　　　　　　　(Japanese Exchange and Teaching programme; 1996).

Carp. For Boy's Day. Running the carp kite along Shirahama beach.

Leaving Narita airport, wagyu steak.

And her days in *'Empty Spain'*?
Fresh as smashed tomatoes on morning bread.

　　　　　…I seek to…recognise myself through different worlds,
through things that only poems hadn't forgotten.   Julio Cortázar[1]

---

[1] Translated by Matthew Stewart.

TOM SASTRY

Your revolution

Of course it would fail. Of course it would be
a waste. Of course, win or lose, it would curl
back into the soil it sprouted from –

mulched anger that cannot live with doubt –
to grow its own shame, its own crimes. You
would often be frustrated, left holding

the coats or the admin, while the ones
whose names were being sung by hypocrites
talked glamorously into the night. Ben –

it's a year since I saw you. I announced
you were young again, asked what you'd do:
a lazy bait for a cynical joke.

You talked about the causes you let go
with a fast, ecstatic, fervent rage.
All too late, of course. It would be selfish

finding yourself like that, when in real life
you had us hooked on your subtle art
of being not-quite. The old half-reveal

twinkling and ironic. The man I knew.
The one you did best. The one I'm mourning
who was brilliant, beautiful, a flame.

On my cousin's doorstep

She has a bell-pull, with feathers
and a brass plate with her name
which is Hope. I rang it and stood there
while in the other flat
a man cried with his whole body.

I had these thoughts:

    1)   an adult's grief
is the frequent state of a child
    2a) thought is our plea to feeling
to let us live
    2b) the mind's work is about survival
not cold reason as moonstruck
cynics say

By now I'd walked
my senses home. I will make an idea
that can hold them. I will find something
that feeds from my hand.
I will give my moments wings.

Rooftops and moon

at dusk everything is sufficient

when tasks refuse themselves

we sit on the swing seat as the sky rusts

bats tie elaborate knots to parcel up the day

slate cobwebs stretch against the murk

i don't immediately reach for your hand

it is good not wishing for anything

even when the galaxies are sparkles on a pool

and it's hard to tell

if the world is ordered as usual

or the sky moves against the clouds

Oliver Cromwell

You are arguing for joy, against those
who forbid it. Who are they?

You mention Oliver Cromwell
who, while thirsty for the Bible and command
was no friend of Christmas or dancing.

Do you think those who feel small
when they hear about your happiness
are the heirs of the butcher of Drogheda?

Come to me, always, exaggerated
serving your truth hot. Allow my cooling rain.

HELEN MORT

Chicken Triptych

i. Factory

My father's job:
to grab the live birds
and attach them by their legs
to clamps on a conveyor.

Pecked to buggery, his arms
crosshatched by their panic
but he had it better
than the next man down the line

the one who'd lift his bloodshot eyes
to watch them trundle round
then slit each throat
with grim efficiency,

who walked home every night
to his mother, along the Rochdale canal
unmarked

following
the water's black ribbon.

ii. Floor

Passing Slim's Chicken Shop
in the faux-cherry-scented Arndale,

I can't help trying to glimpse
your tall, handsome-bastard of a son

waiting on tables, your son
who I've only met in fifteen years

of photographs, who stoops now
with recognised tenderness to scoop

a clutch of plastic straws: his spine,
his gait, his grin – all yours. In the nearest booth,

a man in a biker t-shirt
is eating from his star-spangled box,

emphatically alone. The letters on his chest
say *no love lost*, as in the phrase

there was no love lost between them,
as in me and you these days.

But I wonder where it goes
the un-lost love, if it's there, like atoms,

or layered like stacked plastic trays,
or if it's what we look for at the bottom

of the carton, under the anaemic chips,
holding a nugget to the light, going

Christ, this once had wings.

iii. Fryer

It's hard to believe in Ryan's death
while the KFC he worked in
blinks its vigil on the West Bars roundabout.

He did ten years, the alchemical
hiss of the fryers all night
more comforting than breath.

A wife. Two kids. My memory
skewers him: sixteen,
and jumping the farmyard fence,

that straw-and-sulphur stench, field
running to the woods by Mystery Farm
and him so frightened of the pluming cows

we legged it, slipping, flailing into shit
so, back at mine, he had to remove
his cowpat-crusted trousers, sit

playing poker on the settee in his pants
while the washer chuntered in the background
and we drank Danish cactus cider,

how, when my mum came in
he raised his can at her politely,
turned back and showed his winning hand.

Stroke Ward

Eddie the ex-miner   thinks I'm his daughter,   walks
to the edge of your bed   grips   places   his hands
on the white rail   skin of his knuckles blanching
behind ink   unreadable blue
when's tha leaving lad?   I might as well leave with you.

MARIA TAYLOR

Refresher at Faros

Because Mum couldn't even start the car
I've driven her to the lighthouse
for some fresh air. The word for lighthouse
Faros, sounds like another Greek word –
Tharros, meaning courage. Spoken in light.

After they married Babba insisted
wives should stay in the passenger seat.
Though she didn't smoke, mum's new role
was to light up Babba's cigarettes,
take the first puff and pass them on.

From the back I saw a muddle of hands
across the wheel. I inhaled the smoke
that thickened between them. Now mum
wants to be in the driving seat again,
and re-live how the nights burst open

Into a blur of electric light, how the city
tried to keep up with her as she sped by.
It gets dark quickly at Faros. The lighthouse
begins its work. No more talk of *I could've
done this* or *I should've done that*.

We wait for the beam to sweep over
the darkness of the Med, over years of waves.
How the light circles back to us
like a firm promise. *It's beautiful* we say,
and tomorrow, Mum says, she'll turn the key.

Night Swimming at Faros

Moonrise. Daylight loses its grip on the landscape.
The lighthouse is now disused. I wade into the ocean's night
trusting the dark to lift me. Across a patrolled borderline,
on a Northern shore, the same beauty, same anxiety.
Someone is swimming in the dark and finds direction
in stars. A night sky gives us both *fengari* – *ay ışığı*
in the way language makes its own light.

Arrival into St. Pancras, London

Almost midday   passengers unplug & rise
I spend the last moments of the journey
looking through a sepia window   a loaded skyline
history's grime   how the past clings

Mother memory   a Cypriot family move
into the post-war rubble of a slum Camden Town
they learn to take insults   in good humour
feel the slap of January on their cheek

Mamma's a teenager   ice on her birthday
on a doorstep in Royal College Street   she reaches
for a bottle of frozen milk   it stings
she holds London   in her deadened hands

moments of breath   a shock of light
erases the view   a city vanishes and reappears
sun exposes a new city   made of tears and money
we enter the iron mouth   of the present tense

feel the grogginess of arrival   look up
a clock keeps time   in gold-plated hours
houses long since demolished   a subtle voice
collapses into   a second-hand memory

How can I let you know *Mamma*,
I'm back   and this is no longer home

JULIAN TURNER

Thomas Traherne Has Hot Stones
   for Jess

She puts a hot stone on my solar plexus and is still.
She rubs the Mexican, magmatic rocks against my skin.
I feel my chakras open, little doors in buried parts.
My nerves sing and I tingle. The stones are being rolled
down ley lines in my legs. They have mighty Aztec names.

The aromatic oils are warm and every part of me begins
to glow; although I have transcended sweat, my pores
are active and my body feels recently discovered,
like the Higgs-Boson. She rolls the basalt up and down my legs;
she is a cloth in which I'm oiled and she is polishing

my lustre, simmering the micro-coils of currents
playing in my skin, ramping up their voltage until
I give off sparks. She trims the wick of my fingers
with her nails and lights each one. I lurch towards
the Spa, my head on fire, illuminating the corridor,
my eye single, my whole body filled with light.

PAUL STEPHENSON

The Ladder

It was when the solicitor called and left a voicemail
with the good news that we were about to close
and did I want to buy the bedroom curtains

and matching bedside cabinets because the owners
were planning to purchase new and would give me
a fair price, and would I like the washing machine

which was only a year old, a Bosch, ultra-efficient,
that it struck me in the moment, the rapid heartbeat,
the sweating and dry throat, that I didn't want any of it,

not a thing – or the house, with its tastefully extended
kitchen and marble worktops and island with those
drawers that close with a kiss because none of the clever

embellishments and lavish improvements could make up
for the poky front room and steep narrow staircase with
no handrail – a fall waiting to happen, and anyway,

what on earth was I thinking moving to Newmarket
when I don't even drive and the M&S has gone
and I'm completely indifferent when it comes to horses.

The Young Officials

Thursday evenings, in the thrum of it, Place Luxembourg,
I see them hunched over tables at Happy Hour, clutching
plastic pints of Jupiler, letting off about their draft legislation.

And the MEPs assistants from Slovakia, Portugal, Greece,
bitching about their MEP's inbox, better half, dry cleaning.

And the interns from the European Pavements Federation,
and the stagiaires from the European Cement Association,
their day spent campaigning for more responsible concrete.

First Weekend

We were on the train to De Panne.
Flanders flattened out.
I wondered what you were reading.
You said you were struggling with Annie Ernaux.
I asked if you keep going.
What you do if you don't like something.

We arrived and had lunch in a lively square. Salmon salad.
Then walked along the beach to France.
A blustery headwind.
Bray-Dunes was rundown and rainy. There was a bus.
Which we ran for. Fields of flowers.
Dunkirk surprised us.

The hotel was plusher than expected.
Everywhere was full.
We found a restaurant run by a team of women.
One wore an elegant headscarf. Pink and green silk.
All the fixtures and fittings were burnished gold.
All the knives and forks were burnished gold.

You ate a tray of oven-baked mussels with garlic and parsley.
I had an idea for a new dating app.
Blokal. Bloke and Local.
It was genius!
I needed to patent it there and then.
You said you'd download it.

Then dessert came. A stainless steel teaspoon.
We both looked. Both laughed.
How the metallic oversight had just ruined our trip.
Joked we were traumatised by the inconsistent spoon.
Should write a dreadful review.
That we'd need therapy.

Next day we explored St. Malo-les-Bains. Who knew.
T-shirts in the October sun.
A pichet of rosé. Then another.
They were re-engineering the dyke.
You said you could feel the stress lifting from your body.
We sat holding hands.

PAUL STEPHENSON

New Trainers

You're wearing the trainers you bought in Prague,
the trainers I found for you in that shopping centre,
the ones I handed you, said 'These are meant for you!'

You wore them last week at your niece's christening,
which I didn't think was very fitting. All unicorn pastels –
rose pink, banana yellow, mint green, powder blue.

And again last month, when your mother came to visit
and we went for dinner in the countryside and you sat
side by side and got annoyed with her, on about her guru.

Prague was good, wasn't it? That train ride from Austria
after the wedding, where you came as my plus one,
and everybody, naturally, assumed we were an item.

And when the photographer said 'Say Riesling!' and
kiss the person next to you, how we said 'Riesling!'
and kissed each other as a couple, sipped some bubbles.

How we went back to the hotel to have a quick rest
and sex in the shower, then got dressed for the reception
where we were sat next to each other and did the conga

and sang La Isla Bonita and Dancing Queen at karaoke,
you in white tennis shoes, not the snazzy new trainers.
What is the fascination with little one-horned creatures?

FIONA LARKIN

Costume jewellery won't bring you back

A string of jet slipped
from your hand to mine

✻

it slid over clavicles
to set off my skin

✻

I wore it to death
at teenage parties

✻

and coiled it away
when I heard the snap

✻

I restring it now
for a different dress

✻

secular rosary
each bead an ache

✻

true jet I know
is born of coal

✻

swings light on the nape
is warm to the touch

✻

but your beads of glass
need my hand's held heat

✻

they're cold as your brow
to my living lips

RUTH SHARMAN

Ghosts at Assos
(remembering Leslie Topsfield, 1920-1981)

He was matter of fact about ghosts, convinced
   by the elasticity of time and unsurprised
to see a visitor from the 17th century asleep
   in his leather chair as he rounded the stairs

to his study. And what if it wasn't brain fatigue,
   all those hours spent poring over
Provençal manuscripts? What if past and present
   could coexist the way LT imagined?

This fortress was built fifty-odd years before
   his visitor was born and not much of it
remains: the massive entrance arch, a few walls
   and gun emplacements, a stone causeway

passing under acres of twisted olive trees,
   where the rain has kept the living away
and we're alone, except for a few invisible birds
   piping thinly in the stillness,

a herd of curly-horned sheep, the sudden clatter
   of their hooves on stone as we startle
them from their browsing... Or are we? Maybe
   it's *them* setting off the birds

and spooking the sheep. Maybe, in some parallel
   time and space, they're still tending
the vines and scanning the bay for the arrival
   of Ottomans, or corsairs,

and traipsing along this cliff path, no longer
   crushing the scent from the thyme,
no longer wary of losing their footing or
   stepping too close to the edge.

Beyond the weir

The water's deeper, colder. Reflections shimmy
up the trunks of ash and hazel, and tangled grasses
screen the fields from view, so dense

there's no stepping from the river here, even
if we wanted to. And we don't. We like this sense
of drifting back in time, sharing the river

not with other swimmers (who rarely swim
this far beyond the weir) but with the washer bird
bobbing at the water's edge,

the comma butterfly basking in the sun
and a crowd of damselflies that hover two by two
like tiny aliens in a geometric dance.

We watch one lay her eggs on waterweed
while her partner holds her steady by the head;
we watch a pair of buzzards circle in the cloudless sky

and listen to the sound of water rippling
round each stroke, insects humming,
the buzzards' far-off cries... the lovely stillness...

until the shout. *This stretch of river's private!*
Some woman on the bank accosting us,
telling us to turn back. Private?

Maybe she owns the ground she's standing on,
every bloom of meadowsweet and brooklime.
But the water's flow from source to sea?

Isn't that as crazy as saying she owns the now
we're travelling through, next year's swallows,
the damselflies, the sunlight or the breeze?

DUNCAN CHAMBERS

Polonius

When I asked my father for a loan
on Cromer Pier,
he showed me his empty pockets,
his tired hands
and fed me a line he said was from the Bible.

That day, the slot machines went hungry,
the coconuts
slumbered undisturbed. No chance
of candy floss,
economics jeering from the dodgem cars.

Later I found out the words were yours
Polonius.
Fathers can mean well, be right
and still end up
with a daughter dead by suicide,

a son striking everything that moves
and they themselves
preserved as a laughing stock,
stabbed out of nowhere
and left to bleed in the dark.

Archduke Michael and his brothers

This is the photograph on the book jacket.
They have burned the papers
in the marble fireplace
drunk the last of the champagne.
The Dowager's portrait faces the wall.

Did you notice
the deerhound was dead?
One stroked her ears
one checked the dose
one pushed the plunger home.

My late wife's wedding dress

It was old-fashioned even in its day,
a meringue, a silken stricture,
its train a handicap like the peacock's tail.

If you'd been well, we could have looked at mood boards,
weighed the pros and cons of chiffon and organza,
tulle and taffeta, perhaps decided in the end
to go our separate ways. But the dress hung

in the window, needing only
nips and tucks. I think you saw
a sign of hope, an envelope that might contain
a love letter. I saw the bell of a jellyfish.

Commitment means standing up and saying:
Yes, I will, I do. It also means being sent
to prison or an asylum. Who knows where
we'd have ended up if you'd been well?

Twice a year or so I bring carnations
and sit for half an hour. You chose
to be buried in the dress, and I will join you here,
where pigeons skulk among the bushes and traffic
on the distant by-pass speeds to Oxford, London and beyond.

SARAH MNATZAGANIAN

Dawn

and the sweet remembrance of holiday,
my brother at the door, fishing rods ready
and worms to be dug from the soil at the edge
of the veg patch where the first runner beans dangle,

where we buried our last failed attempt at a treat:
the butter cream of a cake, made with low fat spread,
trowelled in guiltily beside the squash and lettuces
last Saturday when Mum and Dad were shopping.

Next door's apple trees are bonny with young fruit
and Nero's hunting where the chickens lived,
shoulder blades dangerous as shark fins, circling
the fledgling blackbirds in the dandelions.

It's time to grab my jeans, dig wrigglers into a jar
and head for the mill pond, trout rising along a river
steaming with mist, our collie like a hoover stuck
to a rug as he sniffs the bank for water voles.

I ask myself whose stick will dribble with most trout,
gutted with pen knives at the far side of the pond
and threaded through the gills like Huckleberry Finn,
back to Mum, triumphant, and breakfast.

First, the companionable roar of the mill race,
me off to the left, him to the right, casting far
into the quiet water where the drop has carved
the pool deep enough to dive in if you dare.

I can hardly bear the writhe of worm on hook.
We have no watch. Home's a water meadow away.
They know where we might be when they wake,
Mum and Dad, and find us gone.

DZIFA BENSON

Broken Ghazal for Pink and Gravity
after The Resting Acrobats by Glyn Philpot, 1935

We grew up in these marquees where we soar to defy gravity.
If we don't somersault for your relish our limbs yield to gravity.

Hovering between worlds dressed in candy-floss pink, we wait
in the stink of animal manured straw to toy with the laws of gravity.

We sweat in and out of the limelight and it ain't always pretty
no ginned-up bright applause here, just plain old bloody gravity.

Our dare-devilry maps the geometry of our hyper-mobile joints
in aerial chicanes and pyramids that trace the Myth of Gravity.

We don't think in the what ifs of missed cues and not sticking
the landing, we fall to each other like magnetic gods of gravity.

Our old-before-their-time faces were cut from the taut rope
of vitality but now they sag, grease-painted with the drag of gravity.

What good is an enviably snatched waist and popped hip worthy
of a spread in Vogue when our lives grind with increasing gravity?

Bella's other son tried his hardest to fly like a superhero of folklore
but plummeted to earth, flattened like fruit succumbing to gravity.

No more sequins for her then as she slumps in dazed exhaustion
as her only son kisses a monkey in livery for luck to transcend gravity.

We see you watch us hold this rhythm of free-fall contortion in place
as we line up sinew, nerve and backbone with the centre of gravity.

Confined to the limits of the human tower of our own corporeality
we will carry on to the end of fear and failure with the utmost gravity.

Call Me Balthazar
after Balthazar by Glyn Philpot, 1929 –
for his muse Henry Thomas

Out here in this mythology of mountain and night
                    I may not be the wisest of men
to stride heroically
                          like Rodin's blemished bronze
through this hallowed sphere
                            but chased in lustre from moonlight
here I stand —
a protean man
                    with many shadows in my palette box of black.
After I stowed away for destination 'Anywhere'
                      and he found me
petitioning for devotion at the bottom of a bottle
in the maze of the National Gallery
                              he tired
of all those thin, pallid girls swathed in silks and furs.
Here among the great and the good and the bright young things,
                the way he looked
                      at me
was chromatic and crucial –
                      a hot blast of patrician vigour on batik,
and harlequin for a writer's wife. Or watery-eyed and not caring
that I missed the boat, in a blood-red posing pouch.
Long after he's stopped mixing colours I won't meet your gaze
from this frame but
                                his brushstrokes blaze
with the light of a thousand flames flaring from my crown. If you
brave the scarp
           of my cheekbones
                    you'll read it in my eyes:
A constellation of galaxies glittering my name …

LOU NEUBURGER

The Poems of Yevgeny Yevtushenko

Because you touched the yellowing pages
and laughed with delight at the brilliant last line
of the poem about Hemingway
which you read to us
as we lay in our bunk beds
stacked one on top of the other,
listening.

Because when I open the orange-and-white paper cover
of this little book, light and dry as a bone
Yevgeny breathes out
Telling lies to the young is wrong
No people are uninteresting
Going to Zima Junction.
The poems sing and dance around me
dark and bright, black and light.

Because the musty smell of its pages
is the smell of home, and of you.

And the weight of the book is light.
And the colour of the words is blue.

Flightpath

Sitting up in bed early this morning,
the window thrown wide open to bring
the rain inside, to hear the drops patter
on hand-shaped leaves, drip from the roof
and gurgle down the drainpipes,
I hear the geese fly over the house, honking.

And I remember the night we moved in –
that long light high-summer evening:
drinking beer in the long garden
fish and chips in its greasy translucent paper
boxes piled in the echoey rooms,
and my belly straining against its own skin.

And how, when we heard the creak and whoosh
we looked up
to see a ragged V-shaped skein of geese
flying overhead, heading home.

The empty house
the clear sky
the baby squashed and ready inside me,
and the geese.

CLAUDINE TOUTOUNGI

The River River

                which is the first cousin

not at all removed

                to my town's river

which has another name

                but this one

the one I'm talking about

                's name is

the River River

                ie his River

or sometimes

                The River A

or Old Man A

                which makes it sound like the very first river

or Ur-River

                but it's not

it's the one beside which

                tusky creatures used to ramble

and darlings ran amok

                in the wrong coats and hats

chasing each other

                for the sake of love

which is to say inside

                this river you might find

haunches of ancient venison

                (remnants laced lately with trace

elements of sertraline

                and a tinge of fluoride)

but I digress

                because sometimes still

they do say

                River Where the Wild Thyme Blows

(though it doesn't)

                or *O River!*

or

                O Lush River!

though an intelligent machine

                furnished with the bare bones

might term it

                River With Wailing Willows

in a State of Quasi

                -Apocalyptic Abandon

as in

                this willow is losing it

this willow

                is having a major depersonalization event

this willow

                's hair is Peak Bad Hair

this willow

                went to market and never came back

this willow

                and this willow

and the next

                are all totally hacked off

with the swans

                royal fatheads

gone all funny

                like cutting you ice-cold

dead with only a

                talk-to-the-wing

glide-by

                grade-A Queen-of-Sheba

bitchface

                whereas the rest of us

what do we do?

                not much

except

                drip

Cézanne Shuffle

Late February and we're past caring about the proper
source of light. If we must shiver we might as well
shiver amidst cool blue bathers on the brink of femaleness

and masculinity. And yes we have considered all twenty-nine
portraits of Hortense – heart and lungs, what a woman!
So radiant, so removed. She makes me want to blend in again

on the bankside with *Three Bathers* – me, yes – another imperfect
representation of the female form who needs must slip-slop over
to dry off beneath *Chestnut Trees at Jas de Bouffan* – cultivating

a monumental lack of perspective until I settle back into the cradle
of *Still Life with Plaster Cast* to wonder as I'm rocked how long I've got
now and where the table-leg ends and the foliage of the onion begins.

JONATHAN EDWARDS

Boss

So here's a man like a tethered bull,
penned inside the white lines there before
the dug-out, kicking balls with his voice-box,
spreading his arms wide like he might hug

the world. Hands on his hips, he builds a statue
to himself, his face an actor's doing this:
disbelief. He's him who never stops
chewing, can never quite get rid

of the taste of himself. He turns, he leans:
the coach and him are whispering like lovers.
What time is is a number the fourth
official holds above his head. And now

he's a father to this substitute
he's sending on, and makes a man again
of him who's slouching off, with a handshake.
He shrugs weight from his shoulders, wipes his brow,

for this is work, this standing still and pointing
at something over there, this kicking air,
this spinning madman's dance, these eyes which bulge
and bulge, and are everywhere. And all

of this for the man he will become,
the one who's held there on a mattress of
the arms of eleven men, who chant his name
and send him to the sky again, again,

or else the man who stands alone among
the screaming thousands, and can't quite believe
the world has shrunk to what he's staring at:
this almost-*was*, this single blade of grass.

BEN BRANSFIELD

Theurgy

In the wake of oars, the river's mirror worries.
The guard and his dark lamp. Mars ascendant.

Deep in thought, beneath the bowing rushes
and willows that turn the moon to lace,
the royal barge drifts down to Mortlake.

His, the largest house of books in the realm.
Sage and oaken chart. Each wax disc charmed.

From shadows, and sharpened with fasting,
the doctor hears her step within
for the faint place, for the shewing-stone.

Her face in his hands, he reads the black glass –
an Aztec sink to scry the deal at work.

Flames stretch and gutter like a Spanish fleet.
What angel reaches through, whispers aslant,
three steps behind and fathoms from the light.

July, Québec City
after Norman MacCaig

Breakfast done, up on the high stools at J.A. Moisan.

In a framed black and white from way back when,
your doppelganger – aproned behind the Deli's register.

The boardwalk wraps round the Frontenac Castle,
awake with tourists. No gulls, but sun, and planks
to promenade, as if the St. Lawrence were sea enough.

A toboggan sleeps on steep Victorian tracks, waits it out
for the Winter Carnival. A busker is tickling his sax
and an acrobat will balance on top of, then under, that ladder.

Dark magic is batching up frog legs and horse flank
for the lunch *formule*. As many chips in curd and gravy
as you like. It could be France, but it isn't.

Down the Breakneck Steps, knick-knack shops
send kids out with moose teddy keyrings,
and maple syrup poured onto ice, into amber wands.

You have missed Alanis – in the flesh – by just one night.
Up the mound at the Fort, soldier-scalps sweat under bearskins.
They could be on the Mall or the Long Walk, but aren't.

Nantucket

Last couple in for dinner at Queequeg's,
where barrel-brown walls, moody with scratches and flickers,
catch a hand-hewn figure of the white whale.

We have filled our boots, more than a decade in,
further out from the mainland than ever before:
just engaged, our dessert plates scraped clean.

Out on the cobbles, it is island dark,
dark and deep as the Scrimshander's lair, shut until dawn.
Up in the museum, oil seeps from bone.

Houses here wear shingle jackets, turn in early.
Turn a blind eye. Before the Old Mill,
we take the black path for the Old Gaol.

Peering into its one barred window,
you, who are never afraid, ask if we can turn back,
to the moonlit scale-grey road.

Teacher's Copy
after Thomas Lux

Of all the books in the classroom,
Shakespeare's Sonnets – the Yale edition
with the pale green cover – has gone.
Gone with it, all my neat pencil notes.

And though I have culprits in mind,
I prefer to think it only borrowed
by one who might go on to teach,
who'll fight for time and space
between the acts of *Macbeth*
to look at a sonnet.

You know where you stand when it's fourteen lines long –
then you get so lost in its cogs and whirrs
you can hardly get out.
An hour stolen, but well spent.

ORLAGH O'FARRELL

Auntie Pearl skirts the sea

She comes out of the Monument Creamery,
her string bag carrying rashers wrapped in a parcel,
a batch loaf, Lyons tea. Always green label, for her.
She passes the monument to the Skerries dead,
the lost at sea. Thinks of her grandfather
and his brothers, all lost before her time.
Gulls wheel and call in the harbour, she
can hear them even in this sheltered corner
of the town, where shops face each other
across the square, and the small houses,
cosy out of the sharp breeze, hug
each other close in the sunshine.
She walks home by the South Strand,
skirting the sea, its lure and lore and fear.

In the Middle of French

The nun's voice drones on
at the chalky blackboard.
A small breeze

dances through the window.
She thinks, I won't be here forever.
Outside a bus goes up Mount Merrion Avenue,

heard but not seen.
Beyond the window pane a large sycamore
spreads its leaves in the sun.

People and trees are out there
doing things. She gazes out.
The nun's voice drones on.

D A PRINCE

Staying on for the credits

Here, in ones and twos, we settle down
for the afternoon screening. Nothing
stronger than coffee in these hours between
rotas, shifts, night work or pure loneliness
distilled from the jostle outside on the streets.
Together in the warm and velvet dark,
clutching our own reasons as passports
we cast off, the unknown currents bearing us.

Some have to read the subtitles. Some
wince at a speck of mistranslation. No one
leaves before the end, sitting tight beyond
the final frame, the scrolling names
of all who shared. We take what we need,
draining every word, each in our own language.

'... in my average moments'
Marianne Moore: When I buy pictures

Thank you, Miss Moore, for giving a name to
the accumulation of ever-present moments, these inhabitants
of the vast indifferent space between seismic explosions in the senses;

for reminding me how much of time extends like a stretching cat
engaged only in the furthering of each paw
and wily concentration of worked muscle and yawn;

for recognising moments of travel along back roads mainly, overgrown
with self-sown trees, and loose unravelling hedges,
barely noticing green blackberries and road-sign diversions;

for noticing scraps of time where I rarely admire graffiti or pause to worship
the gangly scrawn of thistles, or weathered splinters worn by a gate,
or coded tarmac with a bruised zodiac of stars;

for pointing to the colourless expanse of days made up
of wintery cloud, despite the clamour of streets and markets
and jittery festive lights strung around neighbours' doors;

for sparking a search for the exceptional everywhere,
not in ruffled plumes, taffeta imaginings and portraits of the The Great
but in the foxed mirror of today, inside the relentless weight of my own hours.

KATHRYN BEVIS

How to Choose a Boy

Choose him because he drives a black Austin Princess
 with a nest of tiny spiders hatching in
the footwell and leaves them be. Choose him because he plays 'Shiny
Happy People' on his ghetto-blaster,

Throw your love around, love me, love me, because he wears patchouli
in place of deodorant. Choose
him, this boy, and not the one who describes himself
 as a singer-songwriter,

nor the French one, nor the one who's read 'The Wasteland'.
 Choose him because you're
sixteen and ready, Put it
in your hands, take it, take it, because he's small and
 blonde and beautiful,

because he teaches you to build
a fire, roll a joint, to juggle three
oranges, because he knows the Bible
of your body, its Song of Songs, its Psalms and Revelations,
 because he knows

how to make you shake. Choose this boy because
 you spin together
on Sheet Common, Shiny happy people holding hands,
 heads tilted back, arms straining.
Because when the equal

and opposite forces of our gravity fail –
as they must – you will stagger like drunks, fall together, tangled,
 Gold and silver
shine. Choose him because the world
will have slipped on its axis, for a while.

Simply Beautiful

And yes, we were all horny as hell for Al Green, despite
his great age (relatively speaking), his evangelical conversion
after the hot grits by his ex in the bath, or her suicide
by his gun. We lived in a haze of cheap wine, on a stay of execution

from adulthood, dreaming of: good man in the form of this particular
good man, the Reverend Al Green, who, we recognised,
would not be intimidated by our prospective PhDs. He'd minister
to us, croon in smoky praise of the night we'd take him tight

between our thighs. In our defence, it was this or try to find a lover
in a sea of tweed. How purely Alfred Leornes Green sang to us,
we who were a little lost, we who didn't yet know how to suffer.
How our college rooms rang out in the quad, blessed

by the only man who could lift up his voice
in a way so we'd know that he loved each one of us the best.

JANE KITE

Should I move the table first or the tins of paint?

If only the universe had decreed this a day when decorating the flat would be satisfying and have a pleasing outcome, then the table wouldn't have collapsed and the paint tins would never have been under it or at least, when the table buckled and tipped the tins, both lids would've stayed on so that the paint didn't ooze out, pool on the carpet and a clumsy foot rushing to forestall further disaster couldn't have slid in it and your body thudding to the floor, would not have shattered that glass light fitting we'd leaned against the table leg temporarily or spattered with daffodil yellow emulsion the sofa, the dog's bed and the TV that we'd been going to cover in protective plastic and you wouldn't then have had to ask, would you, what to do first.

More tea?

Uncle Jamie fluffed about in felt slippers
looking into the middle distance.
He brought in a tray of three cups and saucers and spoons,
that rattled and clinked,
then milk jug and sugar bowl, one in each shaky hand.
The tongs fell to the carpet.

He fetched the tea pot, dripping till righted
with his finger under the spout.
He played mother. We sipped, supped up.

Then I went for it – took your hand, remember?
Said we were together, whatever he might think.

More tea?
was what he said.

KATE BASS

Nest

I wake early, a radio chunters between apoplexy and resignation
until it turns itself off. Electric sunlight fades.
How can it be so quiet? I can hear dust sigh as it settles,
memories thudding downstairs on toddler feet
levering open a door to the garden,
whispers from a secret space within a bush
where handfuls of flowers wilt in borrowed jars.
Sunlight bounces rhythmically off the window
Boing Boing Boing…are you going to get up ?
I think the sofa may be snoring,
exhausted by years of trampolining,
cushions pounded into the base,
it stretches out now in the empty house.

Agosto

Agnese is sorry, her daughter-in-laws' figs have not come good.
She cups one in her hand, digs a varnished nail into soft blue skin,
tears and turns it out, with a shrug, for us to look:
Summer rain has split the crop
brown and rotten at the heart with fermented juice.
She tosses it on the lawn, for besotted wasps
 who drift careless and drunk amongst fallen fruit.

In the cool of the portico
she fans her face with a book
and ruffles her grandson's hair
but he twists out of reach,
toes a football away across parched grass.
He's such a naughty boy,
She doesn't know what to do in this heat,
doesn't know what to do without farm or husband to keep.
She cooks in her flat, sweeps,
beats carpets against the balcony wall,
comes round to pull up weeds her son ignores
and to sit under the portico where sun can't reach.

Her elder sister is telling a story, but she's getting it all wrong:
the people she talks about are dead
and she's upset because they never call.
Agnese understands, but there's nothing to be done.

What can anyone do in this heat, except wait
until the table becomes crowded, surrounded,
pasta is served, bread broken, wine poured
and plates of soft cheese, dried meat and salami
pass hand to hand. Everywhere there is talk,
it doesn't matter if you don't understand,
today, at the end, is Agnese's torta:
a broad wheel of apple with an almond crust,
and a small glass of vin santo:
all that is sweet and treasured, like harvest, rescued at last.

SUE NORTON

Return Journey

As my train points north
to Edinburgh Waverley
I hear a litany of destinations
I won't pass through again:
*St James Park, Polsloe Bridge,
Digby and Sowton.* No more

sighting avocets on the estuary
sifting silt, seeming to read
wormcast messages
scribbled in mud. No more
looking out for your wave
as we slide to the terminus.

We're off. I feel the engine
jolt, as if snapping a rope.
The train pulls me, like a tooth.
We gather speed. How quickly
your landscape is lost to me
station by station

the names too blurry to read.

Pomander Ball

We use cloves like little nails
to stud a ribboned orange,
dusting it afterwards
with cinnamon.
Cloves are dried flower buds
and smell of sadness.

Our decorated orange will shrink,
wizening as it releases
tangy breaths of citrus
to sweeten Christmas darkness.

Its fragrance will ward off chills
keep moths away,
help us to think of summer
on winter's shortest day.

MICHAEL SCHMIDT

'80 around the corner now ...'

80 around the corner now, been there
for ever; a copper beech, say, adds a ring a year,
changing leaves, its squirrels and birds. It's been
a neighbour up to now, a nodding bough,
unlikely, keeps to itself, no yapping dog,
shrill mate, no looking over the fence
through laundry pegged, past Lenten
roses, faint still-sweet viburnum,
uncurtained panes and a dank kitchen not quite
keeping its dirty secrets, vapours, best befores.
I count the dunnocks there. I'll have another.
I sniff the milk, gone green after the thunder.

80. It's not about to take me.
It intends to ditch me bodily right here
on this very chair, cupping in my hands
The empty teacup. Corpse? Ghost? A momentary
stain? What you'll discover when you get home.
You'll draw the eyelids over the dull balls,
tuck the lolling tongue in, call too late,
help help, nobody comes.
The soaps are true to their schedule and
you watch them by yourself for the first time.

What does 80 take? Not the body, sitting,
but himself, the person who tenanted it
four generations, what's never yet
been me but now pretends to.

Hello, says 80. *Hi there*. I move my lips
(I must have lips of some sort to reply).
Hi there, my very first words after dying.
It shakes my hand (I have a hand that's shaking).
Its hand is warm, mine still fresh-fashioned
out of primeval clay from the Potter's Field.

More than neighbour now, 80s a lover.
It's not too bad, not at all. If there's still time
(I'm not sure about time, I left my wristwatch
on the bedside table by the water jug)
there may be judgement later. What's to come is
anybody else's guess, not mine.
80's beside me, patient, I dare think
it likes me. More than you'd do in the circumstances.
If this is ever after, well, I can take it.

Eventually you'll join me, on a different bough.

CARRIE ETTER

Cocataté-pu-ché

We can dos-à-dos a little longer if you want.

It's almost midnight. The chimes will sound and stop.
The music must be over then. We hum
Our way back to the hostel, scatter
A few last steps in the stale corridor,
Onto the balcony where we watch
Tide rise, and the sky on the tide,
Slanting stars and those that shoot across
And a little moon diminuendo
Before we're naked too, in bed
With a crisp of autumn in the air but we are
Brown with summer still, and will be tomorrow.

Birds when they wake us up say *antio sas*.
It's time they fly further south to winter.
We pack our bags. Homing. We travel north.

Seasonal

After five in February, yet not night, not yet –
I lean into the view of my unkempt garden
and discern buds – no, tiny green flames –
on the magnolia's upstretched branches.

I lean away from winter, that halitotic uncle
lingering past his welcome, as if he was.
If he sees a bottle on the rack, he'll have
one brimful glass then another of heavy red,

and you know me – I join him. But not now.
Now I cling to the lengthening light –
I will the magnolia to bloom.

KATHY PIMLOTT

The Passing Visit

A friend came by from Brussels and we talked of our dead
or rather about what they leave behind, the stuff in storage,

the binding strands. I told him a bit more than I'd told most,
of how (and I said then rejected, the word *tumultuous*),

how *textured* our long, long marriage had been and by textured
I meant bumpy, dropped stitches, amateur darning. I told him

how often you fell in and out of love and how I left and returned
more than once. I said, perhaps because I didn't care enough

and perhaps I didn't. There was something he wasn't telling me
but the sun was out and we walked the courtyards and backways

of the neighbourhood, crossed the bridge, watching the sky whiten
and the coloured lamps in the trees come on. We spoke of cities,

their pleasures, the comfort I find in the river, how Brussel's Senne
is covered over, subterranean, of moving along and clearing out.

Coda: Tips on Avoiding Religion and Therapy

If it's Religion, it'll spot you, even when
you're crouched low behind the credenza.
Better to throw open the door, all breezy,
and announce, 'We're Zoroastrians here.
Welcome to the Fire Temple' and while
Religion fumbles for its specs to Google,
you can shimmy sleekly past, go jog.

Therapy requires acuter acting skills.
Better pretend you're a dog (a dalmatian,
the least intellectual) then Therapy will be
compelled to fulfil its corny cracker fate,
order you down off the couch, whereupon
you knock the vase of iris across the table
and lope away, one ear rakishly inside out.

MARY FORD NEAL

About a Man

What I need you to know about this man is that he wakes in the night and he / I'm saying that he finds it difficult these days to tell the difference between dreams and / I mean that even the happiest ones make him / That he observes the changes in himself disbelievingly, as though bearing witness to a terrible / I mean that although the pain causes a certain desperation, it also / I'm telling you that he feels a kind of serene fascination when he holds in his mind the idea of / What I'm trying to say is that this man is in mourning for his own / That at 4 a.m. this morning he asked a god he doesn't believe in for just five minutes back in the first house, sitting on the carpet playing with his presents on his / That at 4.02 a.m. he requested that his mother might also be / I'm saying that he loved his father, that he loved him in spite of / What I want to say is that he is carrying more than you might first / That despite what he carries, he is still perfectly / I'm saying that he is no less of a / I'm saying that this is a man completely without /

Palomino

There was a man, once –
she remembers the weight of a man.
On her back now is a white wave,
breaking along the sand.

She runs when she needs to run
and stops when she needs to stop.
As the day crests, she lies down,
weary of weightlessness.

She has learned to tell the shadow of the eagle
from that of the vulture.
She takes no spur to her side.
She has never heard the word wild.

She climbs the ridge and weaves between the pines,
or wanders the nooks of a canyon.
Her body carries the echo of a voice like oak.
She never asked for the weight to be lifted.

Sometimes on the plain
or on the banks of the river
she dances, slowly,
acknowledging the absence of weight
and winding herself around it,
white waves beating
and beating on her empty shore.

PAUL HENRY

Sustained A

The door's eight bells are drowned
by the piano, guitar and violin.
Draped in seaweed you limp in,
drenched through, head down,
tired, pale, in your sixth-form green.
Your boyfriend's lent you *Aladdin Sane*.

I watch you unclip your oboe case,
calmly piece together its bones,
moisten the reed that screams
like grass blown between thumbs.
Lips purse, veins surface
and the blood comes back to your face.

Now reed and body are one
and your mournful, sustained *A*
lifts its head, drifts out the hall,
swans up the dingle where we played,
where birdsong flocks to its call
as if you had not gone away.

The Sleeping Sister
after David Jones

Was Ystwyth your last breath or your first?
What singing rivers haunt your womb?
Do souls care where their bodies rest?
How does 'Tŷ Nant' fill its emptiness?
Who scores the dust of its music room?
Are these Portland or Aberystwyth bells?
When you stretch, do your toes reach the sea?
Is the sun too bright for your children's eyes?

Are you late for your latest christening?
Are you cool enough under wild flowers?
Will the soil ever settle on your dreaming?
Are there candles to light the quietest hours?
Can you hear, Eurydice, your Orpheus call?
Pryd gawn ni glywed ti'n galw yn ôl?

LAURA STRICKLAND

The Leaves Hold On
for Steph

The leaves hold on.
Only your steps fall beside me.
The year darkens, your grip tightens.
Pedalos disguised as swans
drift down the river in spate,
turn like keys in the current

or pirouette in amber mirrors
like jewellery box ballerinas.

Ghosts of spring
                a cob and pen
circle each other
                a courtly
clockwork dance.

For a minute our steps are in time,
one pulse, the cold heart
of a river slipping its summer.
The swans fly back upstream.
We can't. The river darkens.
Bones of a sycamore rush past.

A briar dips its quill
in a whirlpool – a needle
stuck in its groove, its groove …
The pedalos drift and spin.
Marker stones at the water gate
memorialise old floods.

The summer's heat on your lips
must last all winter. The leaves hold on.

Self Portrait in Mixed Media

I cut the letter confirming I'm on the waiting list into pieces for the background. I smear oil pastels across my unfiltered selfie and glue swear words over my mouth. I stitch *run   run   run* across my eyes. I doodle rainbows over my wedding photo (only three pens work). I make snowflakes from a Carer's Allowance Award letter. I paste tissue paper over case notes so I have to squint to read   PTSD   I cut receipts from the *Co-op* and *Oxfam* into strips and weave them over a *Guardian* article about the cost of living. I start to think that hot water bottles are a luxury item   I take a break   I print out pictures of balloon pumps, hot water bottles and humane mouse traps. I arrange them so a balloon pump is filling a hot water bottle inside a mouse trap (I'm not telling you what this means). I create a border with   *Do you know who this is?*   tape copies to lampposts

IAN McMILLAN

Collecting Items for a Memory-Based Piece

The house on March Street in Peebles.
The year 1965.
My cousin Stuart in his boy scout hat.
The smell of percolating coffee which was something I couldn't understand.
The sound of the mill hooter.
My dad carrying a huge fish.
My dad putting the huge fish down on the Peeebleshire News on the table.
The sound of knocking at the door.
None of us know this, but the knocking is the poem, trying to get inside to
shape the morning and make bits of the morning up like you make up a bare face.

She Was Leafing Through Her Bible

She quickly closed her bible
When I walked into the room.
'What's your favourite season?'
I asked, taking off my hat.

Autumn, she said. *The way
The leaves are always punctual.
No, I mean winter; those snowmen
Like melting families held in heat.*

*No, I mean spring. The birdsong buckets
Spilling across the sky's lino.
No, I mean summer, frying breakfast
On the pavement. Those psizzle-psalms.*

*No, I mean that new season. The one
Without a name, the one that covers
All the others like a tablecloth*. Her bible
Was on fire but neither of us mentioned it.

PAM THOMPSON

My life caught up with me and said
(after Greta Stoddard)

'You can go one of two ways, down or up, the skies can be blue
or black, you can go forwards… or back back back, smear on a smile
or you can keep up the wet week face…'

    And I said, 'Whoa whoa whoa life,
    All I want is an hour or so out of your drizzle.
    I've walked down to the shops
    and now I'm sitting in Outer Space
    among the mirrors, statues of Buddha.
    You know, the stainless-steel fountains
    are pleasingly soothing.

    My friend will be here soon with her stories.
    I only have to listen
    and enjoy some here-and-there sun,
    but instead I get you there sitting opposite,
    who might as well be throwing down unlucky dice
    or showing me the Tarot card of the tumbling tower.'

'Okay', said my life, picking up my purse without my permission,
fiddling with my bank cards and loose change. Laying them out on the table.
'So here's your spectacular fortune!'

The waiter brought my decaf cappuccino and didn't seem to hear.
'Go spend it', my life said, 'You never listen to a word I say.'

Here's a map of the Miner's Welfare Park

the roller-skating rink is missing
so am I
and Bowie

floating in a tin can

Orbis Quarterly International Literary Journal

*What a beautiful looking edition! Must get this.
Congratulations on the magazine's longevity and high standards.*
— Anna Saunders, Director at Cheltenham Poetry Festival

Orbis 200: All the best to you, and to Orbis!
— Glyn Maxwell, shortlisted for Best Collection in the Forward Prize

*Best wishes for the journal - and congratulations
on such a successful magazine over the years.*
— Joy Harjo, United States Poet Laureate

If you can only afford one poetry magazine, Orbis is probably your best bet.
— Sam Smith, Poet and Author

Single issue: £6 UK - Overseas: £12/€14/$16

Subscriptions: £20 pa 4 - Overseas: £45/€50/$60

Issue #207 is out now; Summer issue #208 will be out in June

Editor: Carole Baldock, 17 Greenhow Avenue, West Kirby, Wirral, CH48 5EL, UK

carolebaldock@hotmail.com · www.orbisjournal.com

Two new books on the life and work of revered Jewish-Soviet Poet Semyon Izrailevich Lipkin from Hendon Press

Until recently, Semyon Izrailevich Lipkin (1911–2003) was best known in the West for his role in preserving the manuscript of Vasily Grossman's *Life and Fate* from the KGB. These volumes, translated by award-winning poet Yvonne Green, comprise *Testimony*, a memoir of Lipkin's friendships with Anna Akhmatova, Martina Tsvetaeva and Grossman himself and *A Close Reading*, translations of 53 of Lipkin's own, wonderful poems chosen by Alexander Solzhenitsyn.

Both books are available priced £14.99 direct from the Poetry Business website at https://poetrybusiness.co.uk/ or from Amazon.

The witty, wise and acerbic voice of Semyon Lipkin, a poetic scourge of Soviet autocracy and cruelty, comes fully to life in this volume. Hendon Press, Yvonne Green and Sergei Makarov are to be congratulated for this precious poetic gift to the English-language reader.

— Thomas de Waal, author of *The Caucasus: An Introduction* and translator of Osip Mandelstam's *Tristia*

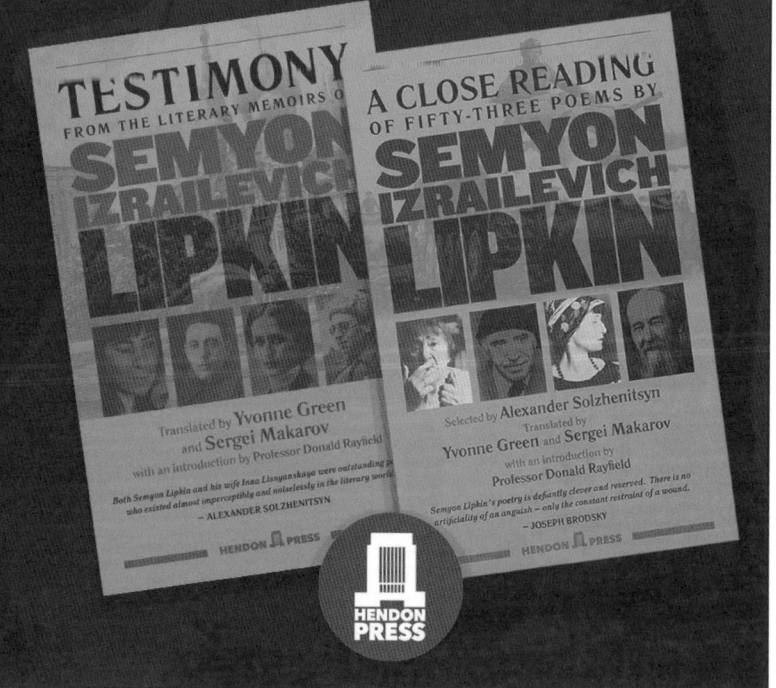

BLIND CRITICISM

In this feature we ask two writers to respond to a poem without knowing the author. This time around **Shash Trevett** and **Mark Pajak** took the plunge. Author and poem details are given on inside back cover.

Traffic Lights

Fifty phantom motorcyclists
all in black

crash-helmeted outriders
faceless behind tinted visors

come thundering from one end of the road
and go roaring down the other

shattering the petrified silence of the night
like a delirium of rock-drills

preceded by a wailing cherry-top
and followed by a faceless president

in a deathly white mercedes
coming from the airport and going downtown

raising a storm of protest in its wake
from angry scraps of paper and dry leaves

but unobserved by traffic lights
that seem to have eyes only for each other

and who like ill-starred lovers
fated never to meet

but condemned to live forever and ever
in each other's sight

continue to send signals to each other
throughout the night

and burn with the cold passion of rubies
separated by an empty street.

SHASH TREVETT

This is a poem full of movement and contrasts. Words move between darkness and light, noise and silence; between the monochromatic and the colourful, the transient and the permanent. The poem begins with a sense of menace: fifty bikers, like 'phantoms', roar down a street, shattering the 'petrified silence of the night'. They are a black-clad, visor-raised, 'faceless' phalanx, outriders protecting a president. Robotic, machine-like, they are well-practised in this 'rock-drill' of a procession. An interesting military image but also suggestive of the more mundane when read against the 'petrified' silence, and the 'delirium' of the drill: that of a (noisy) pneumatic drill breaking through rock or the tarmac of a road. A workman like crew, this dark cavalcade shows no sign of humanity or individuality. They are the black equivalent of the Storm Troopers (from *Star Wars*, not the Third Reich) and they impose themselves with a jackhammered intensity onto the landscape of the poem.

In the middle of this motorcade is the figure of the president. The person commanding all this noise and disturbance; the person controlling this menace. They are also faceless, but in contrast to the black swarm surrounding them, they ride a 'deathly' white Mercedes. Darkness and light, black and white. Yet despite being labelled 'deathly', this white mercedes breaks the tension of the opening five couplets of the poem. For who can find a white mercedes threatening? And which self-respecting president would be seen in such a flashy vehicle? The reader now begins to question the picture being presented to them. This president is being

The poem begins with a sense of menace: fifty bikers, like 'phantoms', roar down a street, shattering the 'petrified silence of the night'.

escorted from the airport to their home downtown, accompanied by a noisy show of pomp and power. But it is night-time, and the menacing riders zoom down a street which is silent, lacking onlookers and well-wishers. There is no tickertape for this president. Instead 'angry scraps of paper' (detritus on the roadside) are disturbed by the updraft caused by speeding tyres. 'Dry leaves', almost like tumble weed, follow in his wake. The menacing sheriff is back in what seems a ghost town for the only observers of this petty display of power are the traffic lights, and even they 'have eyes only for each other'.

With the introduction of the traffic lights, the landscape of the poem changes. Colour enters, the monochrome giving way to reds, ambers and greens. For the first time humanity seems present with the personification of the traffic lights as 'ill-starred lovers' who are 'fated never to meet'. They are separated by a strict regime that dictates that their colours do not coincide, that they blink in solitude, never to flash in tandem. Are these traffic lights meant to represent the people of this country, repressed, condemned to live in silence 'in each other's sight'? The traffic lights flicker in a continuous relay, sending 'signals to each other', like notes of dissent smuggled among a people readying for a fight. Is this the reason for the president's elaborate security detail? Is the threat of the 'silence of the night' directed towards him, rather than emanating from him? Can the absence of the people on the streets, rather than being seen as a sign of repression, be read as danger fomenting in the background?

In contrast to the president noisily zipping down the street and disappearing out of sight, (a transient presence in the landscape) the traffic lights are fixed permanently, doggedly sending signals through the night. They 'burn with the cold passion of rubies' – such an interesting juxtaposition of images. Rubies, with their deep reds, do seem to cradle fire but are their flames 'cold'? The hard coolness of diamonds might be a more suitable alternative here, except that in a poem where colour seems so significant, the (ruby) red of the traffic lights cannot be associated with the (deathly) white of the president's car. The red lights burn with an intensity that cuts through both the figurative and literal darkness of the scene and the reader believes in their message. These morse code blinking, monolithic presences, have the final word in the poem. Though kept separate, though 'condemned' to live in silence, the close repetition of 'each other' in the two penultimate couplets, denotes a bond, a sense of intimacy, which is reinforced by the only instance of rhyme (sight/night) in the poem. There is power in these messages of light at the end, these flickers of humanity; they endure longer than the sounds of menace with which the poem opens.

MARK PAJAK

I used to run home after work. Four miles of country lanes, sparse streetlamps and screaming foxes. My shift would end at one a.m., so cars were seldom and gone in a sixty-mph blur. Mostly it was just me and the dark fields of rapeseed. But half-way back, I'd come to the small town of Broseley – and there, up ahead, was a set of traffic lights on a timer. It took me at least one cycle to reach them; the lights dropping to green or rising to red. Long after I had passed through Broseley and back into the fields, I would think about those lights changing for no one. How it underscored the emptiness of that early-morning, middle-of-nowhere town. It always unsettled and, at the same time and in a strange way, delighted me. So, this is the memory I brought to *Traffic Lights* and, in return, unsettled-delight was the deep-seated feeling the poem dislodged.

The piece can be neatly split into two twelve-line halves, each contrasting the other in a way that brings something of the horror genre to the poem. Firstly, there is the disquiet of the liminal: the sheer noise and size of the motorcade (with its fifty motorcyclists, 'cherry-top' police car and presidential Mercedes) heightens the emptiness it leaves behind in the final half. Secondly, there is the use of the uncanny: the motorcade is peopled with dehumanised automatons

The pervasive anxiety that runs through the poem begins with the jarring commas of the opening sentence.

(the 'faceless' outriders and president, the 'phantom' motorcyclists) whilst the final twelve-lines is littered with the personified inanimate (the 'angry' paper and leaves, the traffic lights as 'lovers' that – although 'condemned' in a different way – bring to mind Paolo and Francesca in Dante's second circle of hell). I am fascinated when poems (and films/stories) use both the uncanny and the liminal. However, it is the latter (the traffic lights signalling to each other 'throughout the night … separated by an empty street") that I find the most compelling.

For fans of the unsettling, there is always delight in a feeling of disquiet. There is enjoyment to be had in the uncanny stares of those 'faceless … tinted visors' or the macabre nature of the 'deathly white mercedes'. But when it comes to the liminal, although there is still pleasure to be taken in the unsettling nature of the unpeopled space of 'empty streets', there is also a feeling of delight that comes completely separate. I would guess that it has something to do with liminal spaces being "lonely" spaces, and loneliness is both threatening and freeing.

'Traffic Lights' is not the first poem to make me think on this. Although her work is thoroughly peopled, there are moments of unsettling yet thrilling liminality in the poems of Elizabeth Bishop. The same is true of John Burnside (especially lines in the poems 'Blues' and 'Ports'). However, it is Seamus Heaney's 'The Door Was Open and the House Was Dark' that probably captures the most hauntingly beautiful liminality – and there is something to be said in how that poem (also Burnside's 'Blues') and 'Traffic Lights' use little or no punctuation. In the first instance, this lack brings another layer of emptiness to the poems – an absence that registers below consciousness on a first reading. However, there is also something about movement and speed.

In 'Traffic Lights', speed is present in the first line's 'motorcyclists' before the poem hurtles on, unchecked by punctuation, into lines of increasing length that breathlessly run-on, with the motorcade 'thundering', 'shattering the petrified silence' and 'raising a storm … in its wake' – so that when the poem reaches the emptiness of the second half, there is a feeling of unstoppable momentum. This "speed-in-emptiness" reminds me of the opening scenes of *The Shining*, where Stanley Kubrick famously heightened the emptiness and threat of the mountain roads by filming the Torrance family's car from an aeriel view, giving the feeling of speed; that the car is being shadowed from above by something fast that can easily keep pace and, ultimately, cannot be escaped. However, although 'Traffic Lights' sense of speed can heighten the threat of its liminal space (i.e. there is no one to help and no time to react), the momentum created by the lack of punctuation also heightens the unhindered freedom of that same liminality (i.e. there is no one and nothing to become an obstacle).

This vague and yet persistent feeling of freedom may, again, be in part due to the contrast created by the two stark halves of the poem; as the opening images are undeniably totalitarian. The 'all in black' uniformity of the motorcyclists, the authoritarianism in the police presence and size of the motorcade, the 'white mecedes' bringing to mind the 1970's Mercedes-Benz 600 Pullman favoured by dictators like Saddam Hussein and Idi Amin. Before the poem shifts into its empty second half with a note of defiance, 'a storm of protest'. And I can't help but remember those one a.m. traffic lights in Broseley where cars, although seldom, would never even slow down for a red light – there being no need to, as the roads were so empty – which always seemed to me a small (even laughable) act of defiance and anarchy.

So, although the poem's closing images of 'forever' separated lovers does nudge the reader towards the more forlorn connotations of the lonely space depicted – the structural choice of couplets both reinforcing this bitter-sweet pairing, whilst also maximising the amount of liminal whitespace between stanzas – ultimately I leave 'Traffic Lights' with a feeling of openness, 'a not unwelcoming/ Emptiness', the thrill and terror of a deserted space.

> *… when the poem reaches the emptiness of the second half, there is a feeling of unstoppable momentum.*

About the authors

Shash Trevett is a poet and a translator of Tamil poetry into English. Her pamphlet *From a Borrowed Land* was published in May 2021 by Smith|Doorstop. She has co-edited with Vidyan Ravinthiran and Seni Seneviratne *Out of Sri Lanka: Tamil, Sinhala and English Poetry from Sri Lanka and its Diasporas* (Bloodaxe 2023, Penguin India 2023). *The Naming of Names,* her first full collection, will be published by Smith|Doorstop in August 2024. Shash is a Ledbury Critic and a Board Member of Modern Poetry in Translation.

Mark Pajak's work has received a Northern Writers' Award, a Society of Authors' Grant, an Eric Gregory Award and a UNESCO international writing residency. His first collection, *Slide*, was shortlisted for both the T.S. Eliot Prize and the John Pollard International Poetry Prize and won the Seamus Heaney First Collection Poetry Prize.

FIVE ANTHOLOGY
Smith|Doorstop
June 2024
978-1-9149914-78-2

We are delighted to be publishing five outstanding new talents, in our New Poets List, in a brilliantly varied and compelling pamphlet, *Five*.

HELEN BOWELL

is a poet, producer and editor. Her debut pamphlet *The Barman* (Bad Betty Press, 2022) was a Poetry Book Society Choice and tells the story of a relationship with an unnamed barman backwards. A Ledbury Poetry Critic, her poems, reviews and translations have been published in *bath magg*, *Poetry London*, *Poetry Wales* and elsewhere. She co-directs Dead [Women] Poets Society, which resurrects women poets through events and online, and co-guest-edited *Modern Poetry in Translation*'s Autumn 2020 focus on dead women poets. In 2023/24, Helen ran a project for bi+ poets culminating in *Bi+ Lines*, the first anthology of bi+ poets (*fourteen poems*, 2023). She was The Poetry Society's Education Officer for six years and produced the Poetry Translation Centre's 20th birthday programme of events in 2024.

PRERANA KUMAR

(they/them) is an Indian writer based in London. They won the *Rebecca Swift Foundation's Women Poet's Prize* 2022. They were also shortlisted for *The White Review Poet's Prize* 2022. Their work appears in *The Telegraph*, *Magma*, *The White Review*, *The Poetry Review*, *Prototype,* and *bath magg* among others. Their debut pamphlet, *Ixora* is out with Guillemot Press. They are currently LAHP-funded and reading for a doctorate in Creative Writing at QMUL.

EVA LEWIS

is a queer, neurodivergent writer based in Manchester. They are a co-runner of *SINK Magazine* and editor for *Young Identity*, as well as a member of *The Writing Squad* and *Queer Bodies* poetry collective. Their writing has been published by *Broken Sleep Books, A Velvet Giant, Aster Lit, Ice Floe Press* and others.

LAURA POTTS

is a writer from West Yorkshire. A recipient of the Foyle Young Poets Award, her work has been published by *Aesthetica*, *The Moth* and The Poetry Society. Laura became one of the BBC's New Voices in 2017. She was shortlisted for The Manchester Poetry Prize and The Bridport Prize in 2020

RUTH YATES

is a poet based in Sheffield. Their poems have been published in anthologies including *Bi+lines: An Anthology of Contemporary Bi+ Poets*, *Introduction X: The Poetry Business Book of New Poets*, and *Like Flyering for the Revolution: The Verve Anthology of Protest Poems*; and in magazines including *The North*, *Route 57*, and *Pennine Platform*.

HELEN BOWELL

Nêspera

I've never eaten one,
but you're plucking

them from your
parents' garden, telling

me the tart juice
tastes like luck.

In my childhood
bed, I'm reading

about your
favourite fruit,

learning the English
word *loquat*

is a mistake:
a Chinese poet

once took them
for unripe kumquats,

and it stuck.
All my life, I've called

myself nothing, scared
of learning

I'm wrong.
When at last

I take
the fruit

between my
lips, it's not

an apricot,
nor a peach,

but both.
You think I am

a gold-skinned
nêspera –

your word –
which sounds

to my
beginner's ears

like não espere,
like summer's here,

don't wait
any more.

PRERANI KUMAR

Kali Lays Down Her Swords
for fahad and kym

I've been swinging from the high paala branch for years, so lipped
with violence. What froze in me was a prayer bead fractured

mid-prayer. A darkling hymn against my father's hands. The long night
I screamed. Learned love was another cleaving. A promise

of tender; neem paste on a scar — then dipping a blade
to the hilt without blinking. That twisted mouth afterward.

And I would've stiffened ice in the winter. Cursed to feel forever
my wound opening against the sharp. Too afraid of love

to move. But you caught my eye across the meadow. Came with sparrowbone,
seal-tooth, lacewing scooped by the fist from the dorm showers. Unwound

the great hurt of my life into a silken tune, hummed back to me
in that long night. Everything you burned to keep me

warm: tallow candles, oil scrubbed from the necks of heirlooms,
        cast-iron shavings,
rusted precious over the years. Without asking. Everything

you burned to see me through the long obsidian of my past. That unrelenting
whetstone. I came bladed

until I didn't. Until you offered up the dappled orchards
of your memory. The cost of heat rising by the week.

Held up a match and said: come,
sit by our fire.

EVA LEWIS

Broken yellow wallpaper / those days

when I would take off / my name lifting
from shoulders before PE
lessons / Folding its white collar
in half on the bench / for an hour's rampant blood
temperature; heart rate / elevated without it.

Then / its little stitches / almost curling off like damp
wallpaper / Handiwork of steri strip / precision in
my grandmother's needle pointed eyes / I would scuff
it / un sweat stained; numbly dry, pulling
over my head / And live with its little
black letters pressing in / to the nape of my
neck / Like another thing
I can, now, think of.

LAURA POTTS

Night Song

After Anthony Burgess in Manchester

Birds came in on the tail of the day
to the evening bells of Harpurhey.
Dusk had smudged the land, the lanes
long as sorrow

in the graceless rain.

He'll remember the hour –
    the saddening glamour of lamps
in the dark. The way the city lit its quiet lights
    below the stars.

And this is home. Old as coal,
    as cotton. Old as the throat
that a boy broke open there,
    at evensong.

Yes, Manchester.
  The little lights lived on.
    He knew the prayers, the silver songs

that lit the sky by night.

How time would remember this city.
    The thousand lost tomorrows

and the avenues of light,

and oh
    the human music –

the everbells, the pipes

that lifted through the smoke
their held, their holy notes.

And those bright gods.
    Over the domes of the dark, he watched
    the sparrows charm and sparkle

    into absence, into loss.

RUTH YATES

Doncaster Pride

The security guard sits wearily
on a blue striped deckchair,
here till 10pm, it's alright
but hasn't even started yet.

And a dog barks, a car revs,
people layer rainbow upon
rainbow, in t-shirt flag and badge,
and the woodpigeon still calls

your name, less mournfully now.
It's been a long year and it's only
August. And the woodpigeon
keeps going, never gives up

like one of the five tenets
of taekwondo. Consider
Courtesy, opening the door
for others, and Integrity,

admitting it was the wrong door
or the wrong others. Perseverance,
the woodpigeon goes on.
Self-Control, not responding

to the provocation of the cat
watching the dog next door,
who is barking until he is sick
and his throat has no bark,

and she sits and watches calmly,
then finally walks away. Indomitable Spirit.

Broken Sleep Books

lay out your unrest

A working-class independent publisher putting access to the arts at the forefront of what we do.

'An innovative, exciting, and vital press in the dreamscape of UK publishing.'
—Andrew McMillan

Take 20% off your next Broken Sleep Books order with code: NORTHSLEEP20

31.08.2023, RRP £10.99

An Aviary of Common Birds is Lalah-Simone Springer's first collection of poetry. It is an emotionally raw work built on the poet's deep wells of inner strength and heart-warming sensitivity.

30.09.2023, RRP £9.99

In his first book in over a decade, *Instead of an Alibi* proves that Geoff Hattersley has lost none of the sharp wit and incisiveness that has defined his brilliant and unique poems to date.

31.08.2023, RRP £19.99/£10.99

End Ceremonies is at times tender, at times wounded, the poems exploding outwards into a galaxy of miraculous imagery and "an infinitude of Octopus eyes".

different theme, different editors every issue

www.magmapoetry.com

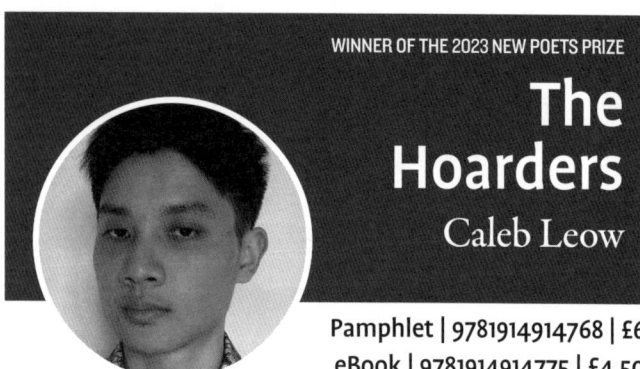

WINNER OF THE 2023 NEW POETS PRIZE

The Hoarders
Caleb Leow

Pamphlet | 9781914914768 | £6
eBook | 9781914914775 | £4.50

June 2024

Caleb Leow is an emerging poet from Singapore. He won third place in the inaugural Oxford Poetry Prize (2022) and his poems have been recognised in the Bridport Prize and the National Poetry Competition. He studies History and French at the University of Oxford.

A pamphlet which interrogates human waste is a risky strategy – but in these wide-ranging, inventive poems, it absolutely pays off. The objectification of the body – whether that is the migrant body, the female body or the working class body is held up to the light through skilful handling of form and imagery.'

— Kim Moore

The Hoarders resounds with a subtle and unsettling music which creates its own complex, multilingual logic, even as Leow brings an attentive eye and an inquisitive wit to bear on a wide range of themes both personal and political. These are vivid and evocative poems which bear re-reading, and Leow is clearly a talent to watch.

— Mary Jean Chang

CALEB LEOW

Our Changelings

Someone's swapped our sons
for the ghost of Shakespeare again

that creolising crook back in the thousands,
to patoisize, pidginify his own tongue!

Be not afeard, he said, *the isle is full of noises;*
Beknot a frayed, he said, *the eyeless furl of nooses;*

Be now a fjord, he said, *thin icy flows of Norse seas;*
Being's a fraud, he said, *the I is folly or nonsense;*

you can shut one up but you can't shut them all
in my country, home of minor literatures, not even

the English who, horrified to find these
bastards, tried lobotomising their children

to take them back by force! This, I heard,
was what the French did to that rogue Rabelais,

first of the *franco-phonies*, a fitting revenge
for what he did to French while alive:

tried tapping open its brain to get at
the *substantifique moelle* within, put

pressure on the skull of language until it
cracked!

Hunger Pangs

The ghost of my grandfather flicks on
like the kitchen light at night.
Like a child up too late, in
search of something to eat, he
rummages through the fridge,
padded motions keeping everything
in place. I like to sneak
up on him, cross my arms
like a parent. Toothless while alive,
his gums go on mumbling all the threats
he can in a dead tongue. But dead or alive,
I've never known what to feed him.
I've never known how to appease him.
Alone at night I switch on the stove,
watch him feast on its
bright blue flame.

Archipelago

isle of aporia   isle of brave new world   isle of calibanned   isle of crusoefied

isle of desolation   isle of exiles   isle of first-world   isle of full poor cell

isle of global power   isle of holiday resort   isle of isolation   isle of isles

isle of jubilee   isle of killing fields   isle of little britain   isle of mass tourism

isle of no place   isle of neutrality   isle of outsiders   isle of parasites

isle of queer joy   isle of rags   isle of riches   isle of siegedom

isle of treasure   isle of trash   isle of usurpers   isle of vanishers

isle of western fantasy   isle of xenophobes   isle of *yin-yang*   isle of zealots

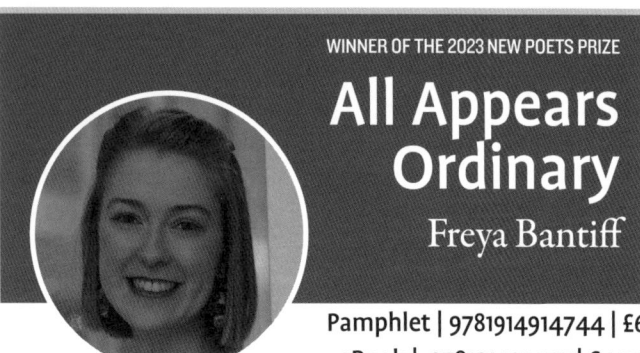

WINNER OF THE 2023 NEW POETS PRIZE

All Appears Ordinary
Freya Bantiff

Pamphlet | 9781914914744 | £6
eBook | 9781914914751 | £4.50

June 2024

Freya Bantiff (previously Carter) is a Sheffield poet who has recently placed third in the National Poetry Competition 2022 and been highly commended in the Ginkgo Prize for Ecopoetry 2022. She was joint winner of the 2022 Bridport Poetry Prize (18-25s) (while being highly commended in their overall competition) and winner of the Canterbury Poet of the Year Competition 2021. Freya's poems and stories have been placed in the Aesthetica Creative Writing Award (2021), Mslexia Flash Fiction Competition (2020), Ilkley Literature Festival's Poetry Competition (2010, 2015) and Foyle Young Poet of the Year (2015), along with many others. Currently, she is completing an MA in Poetry at UEA and will take on the role of Apprentice Poet in Residence at Ilkley Literature Festival in October 2023.

Nothing is truly ordinary in this extraordinary pamphlet, where owls are 'light as an eyelash blown for luck' and where illness and pain can be rinsed and washed away like stains. These poems keep the faith that language can illuminate anything – from everyday acts of love like the removal of nits from a child's head to the extinction of a species.'

– Kim Moore

FREYA BANTIFF

Working Debenhams' Late Shift
Sheffield floods, November 7th 2019

If this is a preview of the end of the world,
my phone is a reel of red alerts and head office
still don't want us to go home. They say things like,
we can't tell until it happens and then all the buses
are cancelled. I count eight raindrops per second
from the single stamp window in the stockroom
by the clicked parcels that won't be collected.
An umbrella shouts up, *it's a hell of a night*
and I believe it, walking faster as I set off under
what once were streetlamps – now unidentified
flickering objects. Dad texts, *I'm coming through town,
where are you.* I say, *I've passed the pyjama-striped
cinema, am stood by the undressed trees and manikins,
it's cold* and then I spot his bald head like the dome
of a temple. Like the splashed shine of a boar snout
polished bronze in Florence. If you rubbed it,
it promised your return. *We'll have toast
when we get home*, he says as we slip into step
and a silence thick and buttery. A student takes
her bicycle for a walk, then a swim. A wrung dishcloth
of a spaniel is carried. A tent floats upside-down.
Nice weather for ducks, a man calls and laughs
like a thunderclap. All I know is my dad rolls up
his trouser legs, wades knee-high into the underpass
which thrums like the dark centre of my gran's
macular degeneration where straight lines run crooked
and there are only eddies of the peripheral.
And I worry I am missing what's important.
Yet he hums, *can't go over it, can't go under it...*
and when the asteroid strikes, when the locusts plague,
when the angels come down with minted rage
and inexorable glory I know they'll have to stay
their blazing hands for the father who waits
for his daughter while she empties out her boots.

Yes

we were at the graveyard, in a smug little village, sixth
form school trip, meant to be learning Latin, ancient
Greek, and you wanted to go home, *domus,* but I wasn't
ready to bury you   and yes I suggested Kate Bush,
scared of spending forever speaking dead languages
to you, then stared while you sang along, notes ghosting
your lips   and yes I was dancing on the stone slabs,
badly, a twist-legged tornado hurtling towards you, tripping
truth impact, just to get you to look at me   and yes
there was the church, its crypt below with all those candles
wish-burning under our feet, where tomorrow you would
light one and I would push you against a pillar, kiss
as you only can when young, hands not large enough
to grasp all you want, pupils blown hubris wide, but I
didn't know that yet   and yes it was disrespectful
and yes a priest heard his graveyard bone-laughing,
shouting, and ran at us, mouth running ahead   and yes
out on the wily windy moors we roll and fall in green
and yes the grit in my knees took weeks to wash
out, like *domain* rinsed from *domus*   and yes I lived
in the wounds, too ashamed to be seen, wore leggings
all week in the sun while they wept and stuck   and yes
I said sorry, though I knew I wouldn't have minded, if I
were dead, and lovers danced all over me, all that breath
coming fast, heels pounding heat, rousing me, raising
me – what wouldn't I have done to be touched.

The Lie of the Land

Though it should not be accepted from a lover
in bed, naked, limbs criss-crossed in promises,
I try to take it as a compliment when
the sonographer tells me, *you have exceptionally
ordinary breasts*, as she smears the jelly out over
the tiny peaks. Eyes still studying
the screen. I tell her, *I am from Sheffield*, find

myself speaking about home, the seven hills
and five rivers as she tries to locate something
I cannot name but might be inside of me – and I
am recalling that time I almost died, descending
Mam Tor in the black shale night, tripping

the gradient of a nightmare. I know how
to look at these breasts as if they belong
someplace else. *Here*, she says, *you may feel
a little pressure*, then she asks me about

my mother's cancer, which grew in grapes,
not one but as a cluster, underripe, yet everything
burst at once. The leaflet said, *do tell them
if it is uncomfortable*, but she is removing
the transducer from my skin, leaving me sticky,

explaining how the probe collects sounds
that bounce back and the images can even show
blood flowing through vessels and, *yes, all appears
ordinary*, as I slide off the table – gleeful
as water running off a slope to its river, looking
down now at the lumps of flesh on my chest,
which are, after all, just a part of my body.

An anthology for the 40th anniversary of the Miners' Strike
NOVEMBER 2024

To mark the 40th anniversary of the Miners' Strike, The Poetry Business is working with Sarah Wimbush and the National Coal Mining Museum on a series of events, readings and workshops, out of which we are compiling an anthology of poems.

It will include among many others new poems by Ian McMillan, some of which will be featured in issue 71 of *The North*. Meanwhile, here are two poems Ian wrote forty years ago, which appeared in his Smith|Doorstop pamphlet, *Tall in the Saddle* in 1985.

More details at www.poetrybusiness.co.uk

IAN McMILLAN

Tall in the Saddle

Just remember

when they crash through the streets
of a village with a name
you cannot pronounce

and when they crash through the streets
of a village with a name
you can pronounce

and when they crash through the streets
you know like the back of your house

the horse may be tall,
the saddle may be tall,
the stick may be tall,

but the man in the saddle is not tall
    the man in the saddle is not tall

Coalpicking, Broomhill

We are bending over
like men after shellfish.
We dart like birds
in the hard November sun.
I have left the riddle
by a frozen puddle
and we are digging.

The field is turned over,
riddled, left to freeze;
there is nothing here.
A dozen police vans
rumble down the road
towards Cortonwood.

A man throws his shovel
on the stiff ground,
the harsh wind clutches at us.
We say nothing,

yet still my daughter
insists on waking at four
in clenched blue darkness

and downstairs we build
on the floor before dawn
using bricks, people, books, anything.

Winner of the 2023 International Book & Pamphlet Competition, selected by Romalyn Ante and Jonathan Edwards

A COALITION OF CHEETAHS
Doreen Gurrey

Pamphlet | 9781914914720 | £6.00
eBook | 9781914914737 | £4.50
1st March 2024

Doreen Gurrey trained as an English and drama teacher and for several years ran her own Youth Theatre Company. She went on to become an Adult Literacy Tutor writing and delivering Family Learning courses for the local council. Latterly she has worked as a Creative Writing tutor at York University. Her work has appeared in *Poetry Salzburg Review*, *The North* and *The Yorkshire Anthology*. She has won prizes in The McClellan, Bridport and Troubadour poetry competitions. Doreen lives in York and has five grown up children.

'Varied in subject matter, these poems are clearly in the control of a singular voice. There is wonderful use of imagery throughout and surprising metaphor in abundance, in gentle and inventive poems that explores ideas of love, home, family and loss.'
 – Hannah Lowe

DOREEN GURREY

Great Expectations

I'm reading it again, struck this time by the names –
Pip, a chirrup of a boy, Magwitch mad with hate,
and there, between the pages where Pip steals the pie
then ferrets a file down his trousers,
there's a note from you to my brother,
Tea in oven, Tomo called round, bus back at 6.

And it would please you to know I imagine it came
from Pip's own mother, who is not dead, but has left it propped
up against the clock where he can read that his tea is still warm,
that he has a friend as stolid as his name.

I've kept it since in a drawer, along with the photo of you
waving from the steps of a coach, off to the coast
with the Wednesday Wives' Club, and realize now how you
always accounted for your absences, always left something of yourself
to fill the gap between your leaving and your coming back.

Paternal

Do what you want, you will anyway.
So you painted your bedroom khaki,
threw down an off-cut from the shop
that used to be a chapel, then with a felt tip
filched from school wrote *antidisestablishmentarianism*
across the pelmet, with a note in brackets at the end,
(The longest word in the English language).
Poems by Wole Soyinka came next, fingerprints
across your ceiling – *be ageless as dark peat,*
run naked into the night ... you could read their messages
of defiance as you lay in bed, you said.
At a loss, he suggested a headboard, talked about
piranha pine and polyurethane gloss, spent an age
drilling and fixing it to the wall only for it to fall
the night you smuggled your latest past his door.
You stupid bastard was all he could muster, but later
I caught him craning his neck to read the ceiling,
looking for clues, wondering what it was all about.

Guest

You came with all you needed,
your car a metal suitcase,

the boot full of booze
the back seat housing a portable grill.

Temporary you said, but I forgot
how little you need to live.

You kept mostly to the garage,
the beer stacked next to the tool box,

the radio tuned in to the French news;
you smoked your roll ups and grilled

your côtes de porc.
My washing took on a Gallic smell.

Now you're gone, I've got the garage back,
but sometimes mistake

the growl of the tumble drier
for your phlegmy cough,

the washing machine's whine
for your whistling.

Winner of the 2023 International Book & Pamphlet Competition, selected by Romalyn Ante and Jonathan Edwards

SPIN
Laurie Bolger

Paperback
| 9781914914706 | £10.99
eBook | 9781914914713 | £6.99
1st March 2024

Laurie Bolger is a London based writer and founder of The Creative Writing Breakfast Club. Her work has featured at Glastonbury, TATE, RA & Sky Arts & has appeared in The Poetry Review, The London Magazine, Moth, Magma, Crannog, Stand, & Trinity College Icarus. Laurie's writing has been shortlisted for The Bridport Prize, Live Canon, Winchester & Sylvia Plath Prizes. Her poem 'Parkland Walk' was awarded first place in The 2022 Moth Poetry Prize. Laurie's latest work explores autonomy, love & her working class Irish heritage. "Dazzling, moving, witty and insightful poems which look at the world with an oft-surreal eye, and show the lives, the truths, the people, who might ordinarily be overlooked." (Andrew McMillan)

'These poems of memory and girlhood are powerful evocations of the changing body and the male gaze. A raw, absurdist humour provides a sense of defiance throughout, and the tone is in turns sad, angry, rue.'

– Hannah Lowe

LAURIE BOLGER

After Class

she asks what's in your locker? I tell her a bar of gold
a snake   my dad's shoes   fizzy laces   a death chime
      one for the road
my whole life in a terrarium   my love written
in cellophane   a little lifeguard on a tall tall chair
her chest

a spilt latte a vanilla Christmas
my mum's heart   great octopus of a thing
inked so we can see what's going on with it
    oh and my heart in the back
    and a scarf in a bag like everyone else's scarf

   a football pitch   his cup of soup
cheap roll   polystyrene   black coat   every
hallway I've found myself in   a lost pigeon   a baby's
sneeze   some lentil bolognese   and sequins
on a trapeze   all the lessons I've learnt about sex
my Nan's first pay packet   a stained penny
oh and my breath   in the back

only joking I say   just some Air Max
a reusable coffee cup   my purse and a backpack

all the things we hold things with
       and beautiful bold
she opens it.

Mary and John's Ruby Wedding, the Working Men's Club

The Elvis tribute insists
they sit in the middle of the dance floor

on two chairs
like they're on a bus

he sways
in cheap flares
    next to the buffet

mic technique
      part cruise ship
      part drunk

I can't figure out
if Mary is loving this
or is humouring the whole club's song

John's hand
Mary's knee

So Elvis is paid cash
doesn't shake the accent
when he says: thanks

    glassy eyes
half-smile.

When John gets sick
and can't get to the bar

he'll shove great notes into my palm
and months later

when John dies
we'll have a do,

same club
same Elvis

   they'll serve jellied eels
   big bellies
   stiff lips

the men will go for the same stories
when they feel like crying

and Mary will pay the bakers a fortune
for a shield made of icing

she'll sit in a booth
at the side of things

and everyone will ask
how she is, how she is

insist on buying her a drink
when she already has too many to finish.

THE 2024 INTERNATIONAL BOOK & PAMPHLET Competition

The following poems are by our six Highly Commended Poets for 2023/24, chosen by Hannah Lowe.

Mary Allen
I have spent my life in the arts. Initially I was an actor (rep, Rocky Horror Show, Godspell). Then, after many years as an arts management consultant, I became a chief executive, of Watermans Arts Centre, Arts Council England and The Royal Opera House. Subsequently I was an executive coach and joined several boards, including New Writing South of which I was chair. I have been writing poems for about ten years, but have sent very few out. This is my first ever submission to a competition.

Lauren O'Donovan
Lauren O'Donovan is a writer from Cork, Ireland. In 2023, she won the Cúirt New Writing Prize in Poetry and was also shortlisted for Listowel Writers' Week Collection Award and the Fish Poetry Prize. In 2022, Lauren was awarded Arts Council funding to work towards her first collection along with a Munster Literature Centre Mentorship. She has published work in journals and anthologies such as: *Rattle Magazine, Southword, Skylight 47, The Galway Review, The Galway Advertiser, The Honest Ulsterman, A New Ulster, Cork Words, Augur Magazine, Green Ink, Grand Little Things, The Quarryman,* and *Swerve.*

Ramona Herdman
Ramona Herdman's recent publications are *Glut* (Nine Arches Press), *A warm and snouting thing* (The Emma Press) and *Bottle* (HappenStance Press). *Glut* was one of *The Telegraph*'s '20 best poetry books of 2022 to buy for Christmas'. Ramona lives in Norwich and is a committee member for Café Writers.

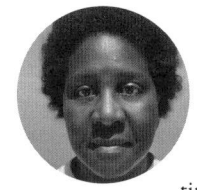

Clementine E. Burnley
Born in Cameroon, Clementine E. Burnley now lives and works between the UK and Germany. Clementine has an MSc in Applied Linguistics from Manchester University. She is currently a part-time, practice-based student at the Research Society for Process Oriented Psychotherapy where she studies conflict facilitation. Clementine has been published in *Ink, Sweat & Tears, Magma,* and *The Poetry Review.* In 2022 she was the RSL Sky Award Winner for creative nonfiction. As well as writing poetry she's working on a nonfiction book about her family history.

Lydia Harris
Lydia Harris has made her home in the Orkney island of Westray. Her first pamphlet *Glad Not to be the Corpse* was published by Smiths Knoll in 2012. In 2017 she held a Scottish Book Trust New Writer's Award. Her first full collection *Objects for Private Devotion* published by Pindrop was long listed for the Highland Book Prize.

Michael Greavy
Michael Greavy is a teacher from Manchester living on the edge of West Yorkshire. He has written and performed poetry at Edinburgh, Ilkley and Manchester festivals. Recent poems published in *The North, Magma, Stand, Acumen* and *The Frogmore Papers.* His work has been long-listed for the Bridport Prize.

MARY ALLEN

Skull

I'm summoned before a House of Commons Select Committee.
Once inside, I'm directed towards a corridor of power,

where men and women in suits gather in groups outside closed doors –
I imagine them in long coats, fur collars, clutching parchment scrolls,

eternally waiting to plead their case with some obscure advocate.
A distorted skull floats between Holbein's Ambassadors.

Is this who I will become? The committee sits in a horseshoe. TV camera
in front, another behind. The public sit in their gallery, journalists crowd

beside the skull. During my speech, committee members shuffle papers,
make notes, whisper to each other. I finish. Crisis echoes from every corner

of the room: *shambles, mess, calamity, havoc, catastrophe*. The skull smiles.
Journalists' heads bob up and down. Questions spray like hailstones,

I jump from one side of my mind to the other, fending off ignorance,
prejudice, lies. When they ask about the money, I say it's confidential.

Silence. They accept that without question. The press stops writing.
I have opened a door, fallen into a vacuum. The skull vanishes.

Finale

I tear up my resignation letter.
I'll do as my father suggests.
I see a lawyer.

When I phone the chairman, he's dismissive:
no, we can't talk about my position
at tomorrow's board meeting.
Yes, we will
At the end, then.
No, at the beginning, it will be the first thing we do.

The meeting starts.
I stand, tell the board
my vision for the opera house,
my passion for its work,
my admiration for its staff.
Then I turn to the chairman.
I am brandishing a lit torch above my head,
placing it at my feet,
where my future career
walks on from the present.
I tell the chairman, in detail,
what I think of him.
I am watching my career burn,
an inferno of potential and possibility,
scorching into nothingness.

I tell the board to choose, between their chairman
and their chief executive.
Choose your chairman.
I walk out *fire blazing around me.*

CLEMENTINE BURNLEY

Transit I

We gave each other new,
useful names,
made bootleg baptistries.

The kitchen sink,
became an outland shrine.
A soapy thumb

could daub a cross
We cast the syllables
like dice,

we were generous.
Each chose three or four
last names.

Maps of another country,
each name, inked
onto official papers,

another life
measured out
in scanty portions.

Each syllable
a search
for another child,

each child
a return to azure.
So many of them turned

to water, we left
the solid earth behind,
took its words with us.

Bolò, njakri, mòla,
carried in our mouths,
confident as coins,

to cross the palms
of foreign officials.

Transits II

Where we landed at the age of eight,
the neighbourhood streets
were patient, gave us time to learn.
Fish and chips stands summoned
new forms of obeisance from us

each traffic light turned
its right cheek.
We chanted to archive
the geographies we'd covered.

Each footfall was a forget-me-not
each sibilant, a new outcrop
Each word in this new language
its own terrain.

We made our ways into new commons
carefully chosen places
known to our kind
where Black boi's spun in trance.

The cameras mourned their broken lenses
As we laid down
the girls we were,
carried like home in our mouths.

MICHAEL GREAVY

Stowaway

A slapdash Brueghel of the sea:
scumbled, dabbed beside a mast
the boy who may be me

won't turn round, sits unfished
spurling breath for all it's worth.
I know that shoulder, wrist –

his damp red shout, weary boat
too painted-in to change –
a greying wave, the wet knot

of his hand. He blew away from me –
the face I had, way I am –
the mizzle and the heave

slip his mind from time to time.
Cloud is brewing, middle age.
Soon he'll be for Rotterdam,

what's lost behind the sea.
Hide me. Take me with you –
just us: me and me.

Frank Worthington Relives His Wonder Goal v Ipswich Town
(White Lion, Hebden Bridge 26/06/17)

Unmarked, ghosting four blue chairs,
Frank spills his wine and soda. A snigger off the bar.

He lets it bounce, once – shaman, wanderer,
half wolf in a lemon sweater.

One touch… two – George Burley is a bar stool;
that old hat stand, Mills.

Guinnessed, we peep through crisps – ten again,
Railway End, Burnden Park a fruit machine.

It will not touch the ground.
He'll dink it Godward, calm as a pond;

sixpence, strand the tap room dog,
watch it fall forty years –
                    pure, a gift, a song –

thunk it sweet and true; the barmaid
left for dead, pint pots open-mouthed, menu

lost for words, Elvis in his head
I Just Can't Help Believin', The Wonder of You

LYDIA HARRIS

The Holm of Aikerness remembers women said to be buried there

On my three islet straggle : see my little chapel
seven tombs in the chancel : seven loves sleeping

wrapped in seven summers ; braced for winter
paused from danger: from the swirling waters

at low tide hear the sisters : singing as they spin
pulling threads like moorings : to the tiny harbour

swimming on the high tide : pale in the sea's light
casting salty droplets : beads for the telling

hair looped on distaffs : of their necks and bodies
arms free as windmills : grinding the barley

new robed for Compline : lit by whale oil
one by one they enter : their stone built prayer house

bow to their mother : their hearts sing the psalter
praise the Holm haven : praise the mantling ocean

One of the seven has the gift of literacy

she starts with a scraper
made of seal hipbone

her finger dipped in ash
spells the full moon

she points north
with a whittled stick on sand

in limpet shells she picks out
the orchid corm

reads the oyster catchers' three lined rune
drags an antler tine

across the tide and not a letter stays
copies otter prints with ochre on stone

shivers as the fulmar trawls her shadow on the heath
she cries to scrieve the Holm

to cover every pebble with the song
knots heather rope and each knot a word

her psalter spells its creaky spine
the pages spill their gold

RAMONA HERDMAN

They offer me the moss cure

Both physical and cognitive (thinking) activities use energy. Try to do only a small number of these activities each day, including basic activities of daily living, such as washing and dressing. ('How to manage post-viral fatigue after COVID-19', Royal College of Occupational Therapists)

To lie stiller than moss.
Moss says, *This is how it is.*

To hold dew steady on my breath
and be subsumed. To effloresce.

To feel cellular, foliate.
To fractally replicate.

They offer me the moss cure.
Moss says, *Sure nothing's sure.*

To be soma-soft-edged.
To be green-bandaged:

a kaleidoscope of rot-shades,
wet khakis and jades.

Moss says, *Zizz through this crisis.
Sigh sweetness. Ice it in rest.*

Brain fog, not me

Some people are born with brains as calm as amber,
calm as drifting down a river in a rowboat all summer.

But mine's always been a hustle-bustle brain,
rushing in its mackintosh through the sloshing rain.

It tsks and sighs and clucks at my lolling body.
It wants rolling progress, inexorable and steady.

It wants personal bests and beast achievements.
It does its lists and expects exact obedience.

Its worst horror is its own failure –
how it runs headlong fogbound now into the railings.

Blankly solidly printer-error stuck, it whips itself
on through its own substandardness.

It can't do what it did. It can't see what it meant.
It knows it doesn't. It's dazed in its astonishment.

LAUREN O'DONOVAN

Latrina Vox
Found poem from graffiti in a single women's bathroom stall at U.C.C.

Collage is Lonely
Any League of Legends players???

This is the sign you asked for
My parents think nothing is good enough

~~Up the RA~~
I'm 29 and in love with a woman; for the first time I know
 who I am

Birds aren't real
Don't vote the same pricks back in on Feb 8th

I have an eating disorder! I just want to feel beautiful
Bird watchers everywhere are shook

Ross Mulcahy is hung like a horse
REPEAL

My BF says he loves me and I'm scared: I don't understand
 why he would
Any bags?

My BF says he loves me but would find me more sexually
 attractive if I was thinner
Love yourself first! You are yours!

TOMATO!
FUCK HIM THEN LEAVE HIM

I broke up with him
YAY!

I Cheated on my BF + now I'm pregnant
WE ARE NOT RETREATING JUST... ADVANCING
 IN REVERSE

And the bullying continues in college
Any Hash on tick?
Any bags?
I FUCK up everything

~~Yolo~~
you Live everyday, you only Die once

Why can't my lonely ass find a decent man?
Beyonce is ruining music

I might be pregnant and the fella's from Kerry → 50/50 is
 gonna be a leprechaun
Bullying is in ur head | change ur attitude

Coronavirus <u>more dangerous</u> than we're being told!
Nobody knows I'm trans, but I'm still terrified using the ladies

I'm falling in love with my friend but I can't tell her
Yes you are. You are enough

EMBRACE YOUR WEIRDNESS
Penis!

I love Beyonce
This is your bathroom anyone who thinks otherwise can <u>FECK OFF</u>

The Steadfast Heart

(An erasure poem from Virgil's Aeneid)

the open mouth of the cavern / the darkness of earth / the lonely night and the gloom / the phantom halls / the unreal kingdom / the grudging light of the wavering moon / the woods / the sky / the creation of colour / the outermost entry of Orcus / the mind / the threshold / the gateway / the bodies of high-souled heroes / the first chill of autumn / the cold of the season / the stream / the shore / the surly boatman / the sandy brink / the uproar / the souls / the dark water / the honours of death / the captain of the Lycian fleet / the wind of the South / the helmsman / the stars / the stern / the midst of the waves / the thick darkness / the ocean / the shores of Italy / the helm / the helm / the tumbling seas / the terror / the sea / the blustering wind of the South / the boundless plains of the sea / the crest of a wave / the shore / the rough top of the cliff / the waves / the winds on the shore / the light of day / the heaven's sweet breath / the name Palinurus / the grief / the earth / the journey / the boatman / the waters / the silent woods / the land of sleep and of drowsy night / the Stygian ferry / the watch-dog of hell / the throne of our king / the chamber of Dis / the Amphrysian seer / the bloodless ghosts / the lowest darkness of Erebus / the anger / the worshipful gift / the branch / the bank / the boat's long thwarts / the gangways / the mighty Aeneas / the ferry-boat woven from rushes / the stream / the grey sedge / the shapeless mud

POETS I GO BACK TO

For this issue **Holly Hopkins** and **Abigail Parry** choose the poets who have made a difference to their own writing

HOLLY HOPKINS

This is going to sound perverse, but the poet I go back to most is one whose wider work I don't think you're going to enjoy. When I read 'Poets I Go Back To', I'm usually on the lookout for recommendations for poems I've overlooked, which makes my selection doubly contrary as I'm going to write about a poem so famous you probably know part of it by heart. Don't despair, if you stick with me, I promise to give you at least one solid recommendation of a contemporary poet, whom I think you'll enjoy, at the end.

Let me explain. I have chosen to consider the poets I go back to literally. Who do I really revisit the most? I've been thinking about work a lot recently: what work is valued, what work is acknowledged and credited. I've been writing poems about care work and, by extension, the poetry which is used in care work. As someone with small children, I spend an inordinate amount of time reciting poems written (or bowdlerised) for small ears, often by Anon and her many, many friends. However, there is one known poet who stands above all others in this nursery kingdom. The Queen of the Cot, The Empress of the Darkened Bedside, The Spell-Weaver my children have been trained to conk-out to is Jane Taylor. She wrote 'The Star' which you may know as 'Twinkle, Twinkle Little Star'.

I first learned Jane Taylor's name when, having chosen to train my baby to fall asleep to "Twinkle, Twinkle", I decided to look it up and see if it had any extra verses. I could see that things were going to get painfully repetitive and thought a bit of investment learning extra lines up front might save me a jugful of sanity later. This is when I discovered two things. First, I realised we know who wrote 'The Star'. Up until that point, I'd imagined it was another Anon hiding down the back of history's sofa but no, here was a known professional. Here was a celebrated novelist in the early nineteenth Century who also wrote children's poetry. Here were her original books, scanned and freely available online. Why had I assumed she was anonymous? The second thing I learned was that there are five verses of which three I considered worth memorising.

So, why am I giving a shout out to someone who is usually remembered (if she's remembered) as a one hit wonder? Once I knew who wrote 'The Star', I started to notice something peculiar. Jane Taylor does not get credited. I have read her work in glossy illustrated child-friendly books where every other poet was named except for Jane Taylor. I have received ACE funded free leaflet anthologies to promote reading with infants, where all the writers are credited except Jane Taylor. Her name is not a secret, but it is missing. I don't think editors are leaving her out on purpose, I think it doesn't occur to them to look her up.

I've concluded that the more famous a children's poem becomes the more it's assumed that it doesn't have a known author. If the poem is a resounding success, then it raises to the status of nursery rhyme and it's assumed to have given birth to itself. The labour of composing the poem becomes unseen. I can't help reflecting on the opposite. How a handful of Taylor's (mostly male) contemporaries writing for adults have their names fetishized as totems of culture. Poets whose former homes are museums visited by people who may or may not have read a single word of their work. I'm not suggesting that 'The Star' is better than Wordsworth's 'The Prelude', merely that it seems odd that the more remembered and recited poem's author

I've concluded that the more famous a children's poem becomes the more it's assumed that it doesn't have a known author.

goes so unnamed. I suspect this is a story about who and what poetry is imagined to be for. 'The Star''s intended audience, and its utilitarian value, lowers its status. I've never managed to calm a distressed infant with Wordsworth, he was writing for much more important purposes.

Of course, 'The Star''s longevity is in part due to it having been paired with the French melody 'Ah! vous dirai-je, maman', via a children's song book published over thirty years after the poem's original publication. The same tune moonlights as the 'ABC Song' and, with a few stuck-on folderols, as 'Baa Baa Blacksheep'. However, I think there is something about the poem itself which secured its survival and for which Taylor deserves credit. It's a poem which captures childhood's overwhelming dark and creates consolation in the smallest of lights. It was written by a woman whose early death, of breast cancer at the age of 40, meant she never lived to see bedrooms illuminated by gas lighting or the mantle lamp. I imagine children, afraid of the dark, journeying through eight hours of absolute black with 'The Star''s third verse in their minds:

> Then the trav'ller in the dark,
> Thanks you for your tiny spark,
> He could not see which way to go,
> If you did not twinkle so.
> ('The Star', *Rhymes for the Nursery*, Jane Taylor and Anne Taylor, Darton and Harvey, 1806.)

I did promise that if you stuck with me, I'd leave you with a recommendation for a living, breathing poet whose poetry I think you'll have fun with. So, here's my top tip for the next time you're feeling down. Read 'Iron' by Mark Waldron. It's a gentle satire on poetic image making but, mainly, it's a poem about the ways in which 'An iron is exactly like a dog'.

> As it is moved across damp clothing, an iron is attached to its user by an arm; that arm is like a dog's thick leash,
>
> a leash that's attached to the shoulder of someone with no arm ...
> ('Iron', *The Itchy Sea*, Mark Waldron, Bloodaxe, 2011.)

Our poetry-reading brains accept the leash-as-arm metaphor without quibble, only for Waldron to immediately highlight its absurdity: if the leash is an arm, won't we end up with three arms? I am physically incapable of reading 'Iron' without breaking out a grin. While I may calm my children with 'The Star', it's 'Iron' I reach for when I want cheering up. It's one of the few pieces of literature where I really do frequently laugh out loud, I hope you will too.

ABIGAIL PARRY

History

It's only a week but already you are slipping
down the cold black chute of history. Postcards.
Phonecalls. It's like never having seen the Wall,
except in pieces on the dusty shelves of friends.

Once I queued for hours to see the moon in a box
inside a museum, so wild it should have been kept
in a zoo at least but there it was, unremarkable,
a pile of dirt some god had shaken down.

I wait for your letters now: a fleet of strange cargo
with news of changing borders, a heart's small
journeys. They're like the relicts of a saint.
Opening the dry white papers is kissing a bone.
    ('History', *Sound Barrier: Poems*, Maura Dooley, 1982-2002, Bloodaxe Books, 2002.)

Like all histories, the one I tell myself about myself is full of inciting events and proximate causes. These are famously easily to spot in hindsight, eg. chance encounter ➡ love affair, but just occasionally you get to see them arrive in real time. This has happened to me on perhaps a dozen occasions.

> *While I may calm my children with 'The Star', it's 'Iron' I reach for when I want cheering up.*

Each one has had a zero-at-the-bone momentum to it, like sitting in a lorry as it jackknifes. (Sounds melodramatic, I know. Having your life changed *is* melodramatic.) One was encountering Maura Dooley's work for the first time – specifically, the poem you see here.

For a really faithful re-enactment, imagine you're reading from a piece of A4 in an underlit classroom in the South of England. The Wall has been down for half a decade, the End of History confidently diagnosed. The world is run by sagging grey men in square frames, though a slightly younger grey man, sans square frames, has just moved into the White House. You are privately sorry the Apocalypse has been deferred, for you are a furious pre-teen: gloomy, self-serious, chronically dissatisfied. You are, I am afraid to say, *not cool* – chest too flat, shoes too cheap, and a haircut like *Rubber-Soul*-era Ringo. This calamity obscures certain historical realities, such as: you've just been handed the poem by a really excellent teacher, one who clearly reads and cares about contemporary poetry. She will go on to tell you all about kissing relics and the moon landing and the differences between the *small* journeys of the heart and the more expansive dramas of changing borders. You will stare out the window pretending you know all this already, and it'll be years before you realise what a gift she was, this woman who loves poetry and thinks Shakespeare's a gas and gives you all the sexy and dangerous bits out of Hardy.

If you're reading *The North*, you know how to close read a poem. But put yourself in my cheap size sevens and imagine these things are completely new to you:

- That you could do that, that break between lines one and two (slipping | down). A verb dislocated from its particle – as shocking as a eyeball popped from its socket.
- That you could enact *perfunctory* rhythmically and syntactically (Postcards. | Phonecalls.)
- Ditto *chilling* (cold – black – chute). Three – dead – weights.
- That lots of things were like other things, and a poem was the perfect arena in which to demonstrate that.

(Dry white pages *were* just like bones. This must have struck me very personally, because at the time I carried around a pair of chicken bones in the pocket of my jacket. I liked the dry and sort of toneless sound they made when they knocked together, a sound very like the dull click in the word *relic*.)

- That things could be both very like and perfectly unlike other things *at the same time* (cold black chute | dry white papers).
- The moon in a box (!)
- That you (as reader) could keep and carry with you at least two experiences of a line: the first mystifying one (The Wall? What Wall?), and the second, sharper-focus one (Oh, *that* Wall).
- That you could just mention the Wall, and people would know what you were talking about, and that funny contract was the point at which public and private histories met. That *history* didn't just mean other people and didn't just mean you. That if you wanted to inhabit the same world as other people, you would have to learn about things like the Wall and the moon landing and kissing relics.

Cue aquaplane, cue jackknife.

Now, when I go back to Maura's work, I'm always in some sense trying to read back to that last revelation, to get back to it *as* a revelation. Or perhaps just the experience of being on the cusp of understanding. If I mentally squint, I can just about hold both in my mind: what it feels like to be both inside and outside of a frame of reference. I try and keep that ambivalence clear, because I have a suspicion that the day I lose sight of it is the day I forget the (admittedly one-sided) deal I've struck with reading, with writing, with other people.

I must have gone home and bothered my family about the poem, because that Christmas my aunt got me the Bloodaxe anthology it had been copied from. We lived in a damp village, and a mobile library stuffed with Catherine Cooksons trundled through once a month. A thick, glossy anthology of poems – eight of which were Maura's – might as well have been the relics of a

> *The worlds [those poems] revealed were not like mine. They took place in hospitals and restaurants, behind the wheels of cars, in media res of break-ups. Adult places.*

saint. I read and re-read, learned by heart, copied out by hand. I found the same ambivalence in all of them: their terms felt fraught and charged and just-out-of-reach, both familiar and other. I mean that I understood them structurally, but their sense remained elusive. Just as, aged six, I'd watched the Wall come down but not known what it meant. (I'd thought: *Looks pretty easy to dismantle, weird they haven't done it before now, if it's such a big deal.*)

Just *slightly* out-of-bounds, those poems. The worlds they revealed were not like mine. They took place in hospitals and restaurants, behind the wheels of cars, *in media res* of break-ups. Adult places. Their losses were not losses I'd experienced, though I knew they were coming down the pike. (I was ready, I was raring: I wanted a loss worth breaking a phrasal verb over a line, or ending on the doom-resonance of the word *bone*.) I had an idea that I was both researching and rehearsing my own future: feeling out the emotional terrain of adult scenarios before I got there. And when I eventually did find myself in those places – furious break-ups, hospital bedsides – it was Maura's lines I laid over the top, Maura's poems I used for sense-making. I have, in every sense, grown up with them. I suppose I've cheated a bit here, because I don't so much go back to Maura's poems as live with them, with their logics and rhythms and precise phrasings. Seeing them printed on a page is actually quite a strange experience. A bit like ... like never having seen the Wall | except in pieces on the dusty shelves of friends.

But it's a dangerous business, re-reading. Opening the dry white papers means putting myself in touch with a nihilistic teenager, looking forward in time, trying her best to feel out the world I now inhabit (I cannot ignore her: she has dog-eared the pages and put Marmitey fingerprints all up and down the margins). I'm frightened by her appetites and ambitions; she in turn would be disgusted by my caution and my compromises (not to mention my haircut). She would, however, be tickled by this motif of reciprocal regard – if only because it sounds like something Maura might have put in a poem.

About the Authors

Holly Hopkins is assistant editor at The Poetry Business. Her collection *The English Summer* (Penned in the Margins) 'takes on the stories England tells about itself' and was shortlisted for the Forward and Heaney first collection prizes and won a Laurel Prize.

Abigail Parry's first collection, *Jinx*, deals in trickery, gameplay, masks and costume; her second collection, *I Think We're Alone Now*, investigates the idea of intimacy. Both are published by Bloodaxe.

WINCHESTER Poetry PRIZE 2024

1st prize £1000
2nd prize £500
3rd prize £250

Kathryn Bevis Prize for top poem by poet from Hampshire

**OPEN NOW
CLOSES 31 July**

winchesterpoetryfestival.org/prize

Judged by
Clare Shaw

 Paris Smith — The Writing School

Entry fee: £6 for 1st poem, £5 for subsequent poems.

Winners will be announced live at a prize-giving event during Winchester Poetry Day - Sat 5th Oct 2024.

Kathryn Bevis Prize to be awarded to the best entry entered by a Hampshire-based poet.

Winning and commended poems will also be published in a competition anthology.

You can enter via email or post. For rules, how to enter, and to learn about our Pay It Forward scheme visit: **www.winchesterpoetryfestival.org/prize**

Good luck!

FEATURED TITLE

Absence
Ali Lewis
£11.00   £10.45
CHEERIO Publishing
8 February 2024
978-1-739440-50-3

*A*bsence is the third title to be published by CHEERIO as part of its new poetry series. It is a book about nothing. Or nothings: losses, vacua, gaps.

From the desolation at the heat-death of the universe to the impassable distance between two people talking, and from the trust exercise of walking in darkness to experiments on the vacuum, *Absence* searches for what's missing and what we never had.

Starting with the problem of how to represent that that isn't there, and ending with the end of love, *Absence* takes in the ache for a vanished god, the permanently delayed doomsday of millenarian cults, and the overflowing life inside our seemingly empty buckets and stomachs.

It dances such a complex dance, this collection: it has serious things to say about faith, romantic love and societal cohesion, and the desolations we face without them; at the same time, it has wisdom to offer about recognising what we have when and while we have it.

  – Abigail Parry

ALI LEWIS

The Touch

I left a bucket outside overnight on the patio.
I'd had a party, and this was the leftover ice,
later tepid water, into which my friends' hands
had dipped to fish out the bubbing cans.
This morning, it was warm, imprecise.
I've seen headlights confetti-cannon
gold dust for a lonely driver's night parade
and the bucket's surface was a slice of beam.

Tomorrow, it'll be a filthy monocle.
In two weeks, fluttering with eyelashes
come alive. Diminutive glass rods.
Vaguenesses that, microscoped, would resolve
to grubby bears with pushed-up sleeves.

It was the same with the unambitious pond
I rushed to dig, and didn't stock,
then washed my hands in. There, now,
the water seems little more than a lubricant
to ease the crowd of frogs. Each snail
an ice-cream dropped. I didn't put them there.
You can see why people believe in God
and His life-giving touch.

The Best Thing About Falling

is that the body's
centre finally
asserts itself
so no matter how you drop

you'll soon be flying
pelvis-first and arms
and legs last
in a kind of bowl shape

as if you were being crushed
beneath a vast
invisible boulder
which is what

you'd been trying
to tell people all along

Putting the World Away

    seagulls caught mid-flap & stacked
like white plastic lawn chairs   chameleons'
tails wound up   moths closed & replaced
on the shelf   pine forests folded in half
& velcroed together   millipedes zippered
    stingrays riffled in boxes   coastlines hitched
straight   hills flipped then settled in valleys
petals packed like parachutes back into buds
food chains nested neatly as diagrams   krill
inside squid inside elephant seal   crabs
hermited   clouds skimmed off   towers
dropped into wells   greased like pistons
    starfish geared   the two of us bedded down
    tessellated   Pangaea eased back together

'the dead crowd these banks'

Mahogany Eve
Alan Payne
Paperback | 978-1-914914-82-9 | £10.99
eBook | 978-1-914914-83-6 | £6.99
May 2024

The poems in Alan Payne's new collection *Mahogany Eve* are inspired partly by a sculpture in Sheffield, but rooted in the Caribbean, evoking a sense of separation and loss, and touching on the contradictions and betrayals of colonialism.

The collection's guardian spirit is a mahogany sculpture called Eve by Edna Manley, a Jamaican artist, in the Graves Art Gallery in Sheffield. Eve is looking over her shoulder. Her gaze takes in journeys across the Atlantic, a grandmother buried in Port of Spain, Hindu gods and goddesses, runaways, castaways, slaves, and a cartographer who never leaves his room …

An exotic and ambitious collection in which deceptively simple structures are built to carry an impressive weight of interest and reference.
— Andrew Motion

With a well-crafted economy of language, Alan Payne evokes the sensuality and vibrancy of life in the Caribbean..
— John Lyons

Alan Payne was born in Point-à-Pierre, in the south of Trinidad; and has childhood memories of Grenada, Trinidad and Guyana. He came to England when he was nine, crossing the Atlantic on a French liner and arriving in Plymouth. He has had poems published in numerous journals and anthologies, and his pamphlet *Exploring the Orinoco* was a winner in the 2009/10 Poetry Business Competition.

ALAN PAYNE

Fathers and Sons
from V. S. Naipaul

I

At three in the afternoon, when school was over, Anand walked down Victoria Avenue, past the big yellow house where I used to live, past Tranquillity Methodist Church, *past the racketing wheels and straps of the Government Printery,* a metallic choir sometimes joined by the sound of the rain, *crossed Tragarete Road for the shade of the ivy-covered walls of Lapeyrouse Cemetery,* where my grandmother is buried, and turned into Philip Street, where I swapped marbles with a friend in the dusty yard of Miss Richie's one-room school.

II

When Anand won an exhibition place, he walked past *the Scottish baronial castle, the Moorish mansion, the semi-Oriental palace, and came to the blue and red Italianate college* – where soon he would go. He stared at these *architectural marvels*, as I often did, and gazed across the Savannah where one afternoon he allowed me to mount the bicycle he'd been given by his father and ride off into the distance. It was a Royal Enfield, and had belonged to Mr Biswas himself. In the end I dumped it on Frederick Street.

III

In a nondescript room in Queens Park Hotel, at the top of Victoria Avenue, Mr Biswas and my father are sitting at either end of a table, Mr Biswas in front of his yellow typewriter, my father in front of his ancient *Corona*. Mr Biswas is typing a government report, my father working on a Good Friday sermon. Somehow I know that Mr Biswas is thinking about Anand, and my father is thinking about me. Mr Biswas says *I have missed his childhood.* My father solemnly nods his head. For a few moments their fingers are quiet.

IV

Both Anand and I went to England, Anand to university, me to boarding-school. *Mr Biswas missed Anand and worried about him. He wrote Anand long humorous letters.* When the replies came, they were *impersonal, brief, empty, constrained.* Mr Biswas continued to act as *the comforter.* His last letter was *full of delights.* My father's letters were full of regrets. He confessed that he had missed much of my childhood. But he remembered me pulling him out of bed in Guyana when he and I went for an afternoon swim.

ALAN PAYNE

Castaway
Derek Walcott

The shock of the familiar
in those lines where you name
the districts of Port of Spain:
Belmont, Woodbrook, Maraval,
Laventille, home of Our Lady,
home of the Desperadoes,
a place of dubious pilgrimage,
standpipes like simple crosses.

I look out of the window and see
a rum-soaked artist at an easel,
a wayward singer in a straw hat,
a fisherman mending his net,
Robinson Crusoe, Man Friday,
a castaway with a furrowed face.

Mahogany Eve
from Edna Manley

She glances over her shoulder,
eyes fixed on scenes
beyond the watercolour
of warships passing
Bell Rock in 1940:
U-boats in cold waters,
the *Maaskirk* steaming
across the Atlantic,
my father a passenger,
above and below deck
the darkness lit by men's voices
singing and talking –
ahead of them, a coastline,
and all the islands
of the Lesser Antilles.

Evening Glory
from Charles Monkhouse

All day, sky smouldering,
the moon on the full.
Now this:
on the Old Man of Coniston,
a necklace of lights –
a hillside welcome
for Rama and Sita
stepping ashore
in scarves and cagoules.

Awaiting them,
two coppery women
with nothing between them
but a plate
of cassava-cakes.
Their voices flicker.
Manioc, they say.
A gift from Yocahu.

Watching the lake's
elongated lights,
Rama and Sita
share a joke
with the women,
ask them about
Arawakan customs,
cassava-cake crumbs
on their lips.

The Black Prince on the River Don
Robert Wedderburn

At night, like knotweed,
the dead crowd these banks.
A tailor with pamphlets in his pocket
watches moonlight stitch one weir
to another, sees in a silt island
the shape of Jamaica.

The Don gives him his grandmother,
flogged for raising a storm with
ear of cat, eggshells, fishbones –
her crime, obeah.

The spaces under the arches echo
with her voice, Abyssinia Bridge
resounding with, *Remember boy,*
you baptised in the English church,
but we spirit African.

Under a concrete archway,
The Black Prince daubs words on walls:
Am I Not A Man And A Brother?
in thick white paint.

He knows that soon
the wild figs by this river
will be joined by colonies of mangoes,
bananas, guavas and breadfruit –
each tree fulfilling a radical rhetoric.
And on the banks of the Don
the kingfisher and the hummingbird
will dazzle the light.

'the burning invocations of life'

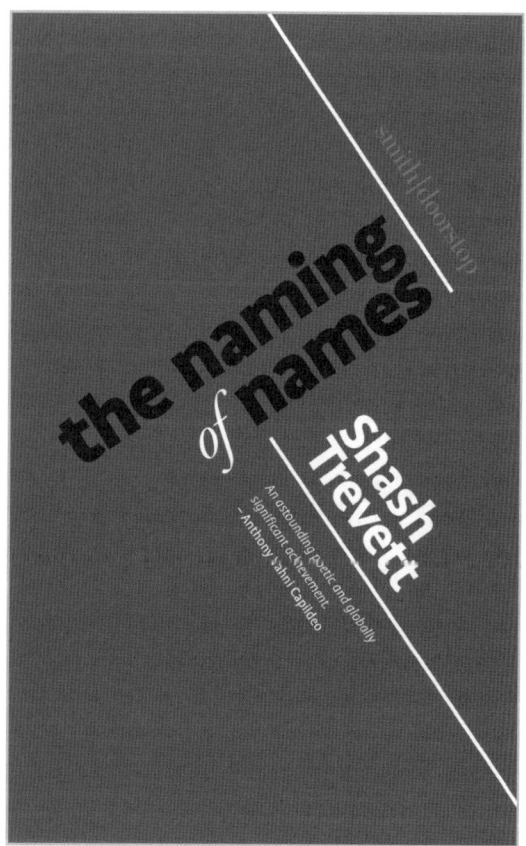

The Naming of Names
Shash Trevett
Paperback | 978-1-914914-80-5 | £10.99
eBook | 978-1-914914-81-2 | £6.99
July 2024

Over 100,000 Tamil civilians were killed during the Sri Lankan civil war, their deaths often dismissed as collateral damage. What happens to names once the person who wore them dies? When there is no one left alive who remembers the laughter they once carried? **Shash Trevett**'s new collection is a tender exhumation of the lyricism of Tamil names: of flowers, the moon and stars; of beauty, music and grace.

My heart was in my mouth and the hair raised on my head while reading Shash Trevett's The Naming of Names. *Poetic language's rare and obvious beauties appear in abundance, blue lotus flowering; but this was not the only reason why. The great lists of names in this book are part of its astounding poetic and globally significant achievement.*

– Anthony Vahni Capildeo

Shash Trevett is a poet and a translator of Tamil poetry into English. Her poetry has appeared in many journals and anthologies, she has read widely across the U.K and internationally and is a winner of a Northern Writers' Award. Her pamphlet *From a Borrowed Land* was published in May 2021 by Smith|Doorstop. *Out of Sri Lanka: Tamil, Sinhala and English Poetry from Sri Lanka and its Diasporas* (Bloodaxe 2023, Penguin India 2023) which she co-edited with Vidyan Ravinthiran and Seni Seneviratne, was a Poetry Book Society Special Recommendation and one of the *Times Literary Supplement*'s Books of the Year for 2023.

SHASH TREVETT

In Memory
for Bim-Bo

After you died, people said your birth horoscope
had foretold your death at thirteen.

That morning you had a bullet in your shoulder.
We were more concerned with your mother

shot in the chest. And you slipped away.

Now when I think of you on the ground,
flies homing to the corners of your eyes –

you were too quiet. And the blood
you left behind when we lifted you

onto the tractor, had pooled so deep
it took us three days to wash it away.

Three days after you turned thirteen
you were gone.

These Were Their Names

What does it feel like to sound
these half-used names of half-lived lives?
Aru-lam-pa-lam, a golden blessing.
Arul-muga-nathan, a man with a wondrous face.
Aru-na-cha-lam, a hill of intense fire.

Asokan was named to live a life without sorrow.
Bavani was named to be a giver of life.
Geetha carried the music of the Gods in her hair.
And so did Ragini. Jasotha was a gift from God.
Kavitha, a poem.

Piriyalini was a woman in love.
Nesathurai, a man filled with love.
Seenithambi was a little boy made of sugar.
Seevaratnam, a child of light.
So many names bound by a thousand soft blessings.
So many names turned to dust and ash.

Balasuntharam was a beautiful child.
Tharshini, a beautiful offering.
Thiyagarajan was one who sacrificed himself for others.
Yogenthiran was the one who chose to serve.
And Chelliah, Kumutha, Kunchithambi (darling boy),
Manokaran, Rasamohan, Thilagesvari
were the names of the beloved, the cherished ones,
the burning invocations of life.

Illegal Migration Bill
House of Commons, Session 2022-23
30 March 2023

I

A bill to make provision for ▆▆▆▆▆▆ the removal from the United Kingdom of ▆▆▆ unaccompanied children, ▆▆▆▆▆▆▆▆▆ victims of slavery or human trafficking; to make provision ▆▆▆▆▆▆▆▆▆▆▆▆▆▆▆▆▆▆▆ about ▆▆▆▆▆▆▆▆▆▆ the inadmissibility of certain protection and human rights ▆▆▆▆▆▆▆▆▆▆▆▆▆▆▆▆▆▆▆▆ of persons entering the United Kingdom. ▆▆

II

A bill to ▆▆▆ make provision ▆▆▆ about the inadmissibility of ▆▆▆▆▆▆▆▆▆▆▆▆▆▆▆▆▆▆▆▆▆▆▆▆▆▆▆▆▆▆ safe and legal routes ▆▆▆▆▆▆▆▆▆

III

A bill to make provision for ▆▆▆▆▆▆▆▆▆▆▆▆▆▆▆▆▆▆▆▆▆▆▆▆▆▆▆▆▆▆▆▆▆▆▆ detention ▆▆

When David Heard
after Thomas Tomkins

"When David heard
that Absalon was dead, he went
up to his chamber and wept".

It begins quietly. The trebles leading,
the altos and then the tenors joining.
It is sorrow. Wave after wave
borne on a wall of homophonic sound.
The contrapuntal boom of the basses,
a thud from the heart of a king and a father.

"Oh my son, my son, my son". Repeated
over twenty-five bars. A mind unable
to move beyond the keening of his name.
"Absalon, my son" plucked from the stave
by voices harmonised in lament and regret.

"Would God I had died for thee".
The interval from the 'would' to 'God'
begins as a rising minor 3rd, and retreats,
almost immediately, to a rising semitone.
There it hangs, a father in despair.

The tessitura rises, the rhythm is charged
as this private grief moves from the bedchamber
to flow around the quire in song.
Then the music ebbs, surprises
the listener, shifts from the minor

to coalesce around the major tonic.
The other side of pain.
Pleasing to the ear, but maybe,
not to the mind. Would God
all grief run a course like this.

'protected by brambles and gorse'

The Luck
Jane Routh

Paperback | 978-1-914914-87-4 | £10.99
eBook | 978-1-914914-88-1 | £6.99
July 2024

After lockdowns have swept calendars clear, leaf-fall, early sunrise and gales are Jane Routh's measures of time, as she goes about her tasks in the hill pasture and woodlands where she has the luck to live.

With sharp, lyrical description and down-to earth understanding, her poems consider the flora and fauna around her, formative moments and lifespans – as well as the dead who won't be forgotten. Her elegant and informed writing conveys a sense of belonging in a particular place and the care for its future, carrying a universal resonance.

The Luck is **Jane Routh**'s fifth collection of poetry Smith|Doorstop has published. *Circumnavigation* won the Poetry Business Book and Pamphlet competition in 2002 and was shortlisted for the Forward First Collection Prize; *Teach Yourself Mapmaking* was a PBS Recommendation. Individual poems have won several competitions including the Academi Cardiff International and Strokestown International Competitions, and the Long Poem Prize from Second Light. She lives on the northern edge of the Forest of Bowland, where she looks after Ancient Semi-Natural Woodland and new woods she has planted for the future. Smith|Doorstop also published *Falling into Place*, her prose book about a year's life and work in this area of north Lancashire.

JANE ROUTH

It's a mast year again

and the oaks of course are bigger than last time so there's more
acorns everywhere underfoot like skating on ball-bearings

rooks are flying off with them squirrels are hoarding them mice
fatten and jays stab them down into the lawn and check sightlines

some already anchored upright their fat white rootlets
reaching for good earth to tow the nut down into dark safety

I ask you to help sweep up the leaves and you bring me
a washing-up bowl full of acorns where do I want them

not in the compost not in the leaf bin why not back under an oak
close in by the trunk where low light will stop a plague of seedlings

but you take them down the field scatter optimism with them
that they'll get away protected by brambles and gorse

and I rake the leaves lightly dull greens and yellows from the ash
grey brown from the oak leaving the shiny bright nuts on the ground

picking out twigs one ash with a blackened leaf and leaf stem
nothing dry about it nothing seasonal about disease   that one I burn

Idle talk,

        that's all it was, my saying
into the evening's fireside silence, 'Wouldn't it
be lovely to be able to do it all again – yet
knowing everything you know now?'
My mind had been wandering through the woods,
the cleared bramble patch, the hornbeams to plant

and how much better a start they'll have
than my first plantings did, before I knew
how many deer there are, the damage they do,
before I could guess at a tree's upthrust and spread
and all its attendant alterations to light and air,
to drainage and woodland floor.

You didn't reply for a while. A log shifted
in the fire; a yellow flare. When you did,
it was to ask what it was I'd want to be different
– but all I could say to you was 'Nothing'. There's nothing
I'd want any different from this: red-berried guelder
I planted, ever-flowering gorse that I didn't,

the old woods and new going their own ways now –
so I can laugh about starting back then with sketch-plans
and lists, to find land working on its own terms, not ours
but generously: daily unfolding some new joy
for short-lived creatures like us to uncover,
with our idle thoughts and a fireside to think them by.

JANE ROUTH

Out of time

Days have detached themselves from the calendar
repeating like the tick at the end of old 78s
and the weather colludes: the third week of sun
or the fourth? – blossom on wild cherries
against always a background of blue.

My watch has stopped at 15.35. The battery sort.   *14th April 2020*
No market. No stallholder who could fix it.
My father gave me my mother's wind-up watch
warning it would be no use: one of those
that would only go on the wrist it knew.

Meantime birch trees relax into green haze,
– one long inbreath of catkins, leaves, expansion and seeds
before their outbreath shedding and regathering.
Lambs on the hill slow down and fatten. Ash hold back
but beech shed last year's browns, make ready

– all that stuff, and bluebells and early purples
and going by the light and listening to your body clock
would make it feel like a holiday   but for the thin fog
of anxiety that doesn't disperse and   yes
this   guilt   at any joy

Two million confirmed infections worldwide

The dead never leave III

The dead do not leave. Everywhere, look:
they've strewed so much of themselves around.
That pink-flowered sheet you've just spread
under the hedge to catch clippings, that's theirs.
Your old green jumper that still fits – every
stitch of it was slipped round their fingers.
They gave you that glass when you left home.
A carved wooden trunk, boys' adventure stories
– their clutter so taken for granted, so much a part
of your own everyday, you don't notice it

until it catches you out, appearing from nowhere
like the leather key-case in your car door pocket,
dropped there after you'd locked their house
– cleared and cleaned one last time – and surfacing
only when your car fails its MOT and goes for scrap,
or like the phrase that isn't yours, but theirs and
unremarked until their neighbour tells you, you sound
just like your father. Come across their handwriting
and here they are, their inimitable selves loud and clear
with a copperplate flourish. Let alone their words.

The verge,

that passive sweep of rough grass where tractor drivers
pull over – not to let you by but because it's the spot
they pick up a phone signal – has recast itself
after this gussey weather, *overnight* I want to say
at the suddenness of the old hedge throwing up six-foot hazels,
blackthorn roots claiming ground for knee-high spikes
and brambles splayed over, under and across everything,
clusters of red berries already gleaming, the odd black one
if you'd shoulder in through nettles and wade
a thigh-high wild raspberry thicket among hardheads
and tufted vetch and great willow herb,
a patch of palest cream honeysuckle the evening topnote
over damp and rank verdure and crushed fern.

That shock of growth: how can I not have watched it
wilding up this year – it's as if I'd gone missing from my life,
looking away, looking inwards, occupied with human disease,
not even registering when the delivery driver complained
You people, you've no idea how to look after hedges round here.
No one can cut before September, I told him, a man
on the side of vans, not birds, insects, seeds.
We have it all in hand, we think: next month, Kenny
will be along with the flail, tyres flattening the undergrowth
while he squares the old hedge back to an orderly line.
My back turned so briefly and I see
how loose a grip we have on a world on the verge
of turning back to purposes of its own instead of ours.

An "Arctic maritime airmass impact"

Where your boots had tracked through snow,
a dead pheasant: not fox, not badger –
only one side of the breast eaten away,
the killer too small to make off with its kill.
Maybe the feral cat you thought you saw
evaporating into shadow last week.

Next morning an eviscerated bloody mess
dragged a dozen paces off, vivid on snow.
No sign of the head. Late in the day
a pair of crows en route to their roost
paused on the ash crown, parleyed,
dropped down to their undertaking.

Cleared of bright feathers, how tidy they left it:
attached to the bare pink beads of a spine
pale leg bones dangled scaly grey claws
at ungainly angles – like legs which had danced
and clattered on stage before a puppeteer
had laid them and their act aside.

As snow melted, the feathers spread –
small creatures cleaning off even the skin
that had held them, before worms seize each shaft
to tug down into earth. The legs lay
as if waiting for their next performance but
their next act – like the snow's – was to vanish.

LITTLE BETTY 2024

   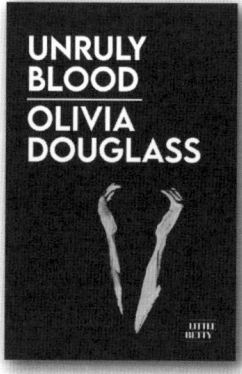 

Like a funeral held in a bouncy castle Caroline Bird	A delicious mini-biography of the mythic figure Rishi Dastidar	A work of claustrophobia, heat and longing Susannah Dickey	These are deep, intriguing, dangerous poems Brian Eno	Embodies trans joy and trans vulnerability Golnoosh Nour

Launching 23rd June, 6pm at the Last Word Festival, Roundhouse, London
Curated by Anja Konig & Gboyega Odubanjo | Bad Betty Press | badbettypress.com

Ó Faoláin Short Story Competition

Open for entries 1 May – 31 August | *www.munsterlit.ie*

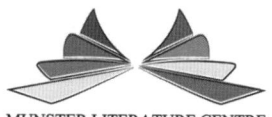

Word limit: 3,000
Closing date: 31st July
Entry fee: €19

Fool for Poetry Chapbook Competition

Open for entries 1 June – 31 August | *www.munsterlit.ie*

Page limit: 16 – 24
Closing date: 31st August
Entry fee: €25

SOUTHWORD
editions

REVIEWS

by: Angela Cleland, Belinda Cooke, Ian McMillan, Jonathan Davidson, Edmund Prestwich, James Caruth, Suzanne Conway and Theophilus Kwek

ANGELA CLELAND

Sarala Estruch, *After All We Have Travelled*, 72pp, £10.99 Nine Arches Press

Amy Acre, *Mothersong*, 80pp, £9.99 Bloomsbury Poetry

Isabel Galleymore, *Baby Schema*, 72pp, £11.99 Carcanet Poetry

After All We Have Travelled, is **Salara Estruch**'s debut collection. In the introductory poem 'On Sound', Estruch primes us to listen closely – 'They say no / sound // is ever lost', that each:

> ... reverberates
> indefinitely / at a
> frequency / our ears
> cannot touch / but
> the body / hears

As we move through the collection, we are on the lookout for these reverberations – and we find them everywhere.

In 'A Love Story, or The English Dream', a couple arrive in England as 'immigrants carrying a larger suitcase / of connotations'. Through the first section, Estruch goes on to set the loom for the book, with closely imagined scenes from her family's past underpinning how we read the poems that follow and establishing the symbolism that runs through the collection.

As Estruch charts her family's story, the poems speak to each other across time and space, via sharing of titles, as in Kesh (I) and Kesh (II), by reflecting or offsetting themes, or sharing motifs. An example is the motif of the rose. In the poem 'Freight' the rose appears as a symbol of Englishness, whiteness and perceived superiority, with the poet concluding that she 'could never be … a real English rose'. Across the collection the meaning of the rose is transformed, until in the numbered list poem 'I research the origins of the modern rose and discover', its hybridisation is presented as a celebration of mixed heritage, 'Flower with a thousand faces, six thousand five hundred tongues'.

Often, information Estruch has seeded earlier in the book is key to our full understanding of a poem. She uses this to great effect in 'My Indian Grandmother'. When the grandmother turns up 'six weeks after my father's death', and '… is a million questions, / wants to know my favourite / everything at the Pick N Mix aisle', we know more than the young narrator of the poem – we know why 'In the kitchen, the kettle screams', which lends us a sort of sense of reader omniscience. This interconnectedness provides a richness to the narrative which builds poem on poem.

Working with a family past necessarily requires a degree of fictionalisation and Estruch handles this expertly using varied form and texture. The poem 'Starting from a Dream, 1983', which has a sub-poem trickling diagonally through it 'a touch away from breaking / through' is cinematic and understated. As we move through the collection there is remarkable formal variety – prose poetry, poems which straddle the page, poems shot through with white space and 'Camera Lucida', a photo album poem, its parts arranged on the pages in boxes, text fading as it progresses.

Estruch is very present in the poems throughout. For

Working with a family past necessarily requires a degree of fictionalisation and Estruch handles this expertly using varied form and texture.

example, in 'Grandfather Speaks (via Audio Recording)' she says:

> ... When a favourite poet says be shameless
> about your shame, he means this moment. He means
> me sitting with my grandfather's unspoken words
> in my ear and willing him to say them ...

The spoken and the unspoken past is key to the poet's journey. We are reminded of lines from earlier in the book:

> ... Sure enough,
> my grandmother starts to speak. I collect the words
>
> like threads in the web that holds me, has held me
> my entire life,

This acknowledgement of the poet's responsibility towards her subject matter, gives the work a sense of controlled vulnerability.

Estruch ends the collection with a Ghazal, traditionally associated with love and separation. The book is ultimately the search for a father, both lost and still there all along. While the poem ends with the question, 'Father, and Poet. Tell me honestly. What are you – what am I – trying to say?', elsewhere in this final section acceptance steps into the place of rejection, belonging replaces strangeness, and there is a satisfying sense that we have arrived at some kind of destination.

Engaging with questions of self, family, identity and cultural belonging, *For All We Have Travelled* is a confident, cohesive and moving debut, and it leaves you with the sense that a great deal of time and distance have been traversed within the confines of its narrow spine.

Amy Acre's debut *Mothersong* is a book equally rich in texture and colour. But if Estruch's is a tapestry, Acre's is a punk collage. It's alive, grounded and granular. Although the experiences Acre presents to us are necessarily filtered and crafted, the overall effect is one of rawness and closeness to the experience.

Again, the poet's loss of her father at a young age bleeds through the collection, but Acre handles it in a very different way. There is history here, but it feels less looked back upon and more relived – as if *Mothersong* pulls opens the ribcage of the present moment and finds the past muddled in with the guts of now.

Poems like 'Azrael' and 'Dance on my Grave' illustrate how becoming a mother and the experience of early motherhood can act as a lightning rod for memory and can force us to relive and recontextualize our own formative childhood and teen experiences in the light of the new perspective of parenthood.

Acre's poems, in particular those which look into the past, are rich with cultural references and texture. 'Every Girl Knows' is almost frantic with it: 'tube purgatory, blockbusters, park bench, trocadero', while 'The Year of the Horse' carefully mines phrases first recorded in print in 1990.

Like *For All We Have Travelled*, *Mothersong* is formally varied. 'See Also' is a hilarious and incisive poem assembled using found text pertaining to definitions of the words 'mother' and 'father' and all their associated variations and diminutives. 'Hip, Hip, Hooray!' takes the form of imagined labels for figures in a painting.

Many of these poems talk about the darker side of becoming a mother, and look you straight in the eye while they do it. 'Atheism', a prose poem about pelvic prolapse, begins: 'dear lord, fix my broken vagina that I may climb the tree of longing.' The last phrase in this poem 'I know I am in here somewhere' might be the collection's subtitle, and could well be printed on a t-shirt to be gifted to new mothers everywhere. It speaks to a different sort of search for self – the need for reconnection. It's echoed in 'Ali Talks me Through the Multiverse' with the phrase 'Before we were mothers, we were people'. 'Daddy Pig' is another poem which addresses loss of self, ending with the heartbreaking:

> it is terrible and confusing
> to be the same story day after day
> to look over the edge and never smash
> you see a piece of yourself on the ground

Many of these poems talk about the darker side of becoming a mother, and look you straight in the eye while they do it.

and just leave it there
maybe you'll come back to it later

There are multiple moments in this collection when the wisdom offered has the ring of weird things children ask you, or tell you with confidence. This adds to the sense that the poet is concerned with the messy nature of memory and understanding. The poem 'Maybe', is a good example of how we revise our understanding of situations over time. The child in the poem doesn't know 'if people remove / their clothes when they want to remove their skin.'

A highlight for me is 'Reckless', a poem which speaks of the necessity of vulnerability in the act of loving. It opens with a mouthwatering line-break paired with an image that leaves you painfully minty fresh:

the thrill of being
skinless, opening
the submarine
window, peeling
a two-minute egg

This wildness and openness to the potential for damage feels so central to the human experience and to this collection, as is the sense that it is somehow all worth it. As the final poem 'T - Minus Zero' concludes:

when she comes
         you won't remember if she cried
because
look
look at the day
arriving
         someone is here

Mothersong doesn't feel like a debut. Acre deals unselfconsciously with the emotional and physical trauma of beginnings and endings, painting a vivid portrait of the raw edges of motherhood and loss. This book is uncompromising, darkly humorous, and gets bonus points from me for containing a poem that references the film *Alien*.

Isabel Galleymore's second collection, *Baby Schema*, is a book concerned with the tensions between the urge to procreate and the desire to preserve the environment.

Galleymore engages with the natural world with the down-on-your-knees closeness of a naturalist. Some of the poems, such as 'Busy, busy' sent me reaching for my Norman MacCaig. This is a piece that looks simple until you begin to unpick the craft:

Don't you just love it when you're held up
by a slug? On the path,
this hunkling of fudge
is plugging away at the task
         of moving herself,

'Hunkling of fudge' is tremendous, as are the playful multiple-meanings in 'held up'. Slug as delay? Slug as highwayman? Slug as emotional support? But dig in further and we also see the care with which Galleymore has chosen every word. The repeated 'uh' sound in 'just', 'love', 'up', 'hunkling', 'fudge', 'plugging' not only adds music here, but is what I think of as an 'up' sound, propping us up each time it occurs, like a someone keeping a balloon in the air by patting it on the bottom. I love poems like this, where the craft is unobtrusive, but hard working.

Baby Schema is an absolute box of delights for lovers of a deftly deployed line break. A prime example is the poem 'Like Nothing Else':

Why would you have a child, the toad
in the wet grass asks,
the earwig asks
as you carry each away from where you dig –
it's something to do
with love, you're meant to
say ...

The break on 'toad' is hilarious, but look at how Galleymore leaves an extra layer of meaning hanging on the lines 'it's something to do' and '... you're meant

Galleymore engages with the natural world with the down-on-your-knees closeness of a naturalist.

to'. Coming soon to a workshop near you!

Thematically, in many poems, two things are happening at once. In 'Release' a tree frog species is a period starting, but it's not that one thing is standing in for the other, so much as things are each other – thoughts are amalgamated. This slippery approach works well to convey the complexity of the question – how can the biological imperative or social expectation to breed be reconciled with the ecological impact of the decision?

Galleymore comes at her subject matter from multiple interesting angles. 'Because' is a fable about trying to find good reasons for procreating, 'Fable' a surreal overpopulation nightmare. 'Chosen' addresses the difficult question of how you can choose existence for another being unequipped to make the choice itself. A potential person exists as a 'scratching / in the wall', like mice.

The collection ends with 'Birdsong', a surreal piece in which the speaker finds their mouth is gone.

A surprise.
The bird with its
back to me as if
I could be the background.

It's a surreal, yet hopeful poem. Ultimately, we are left asking can we be the background? Can we put our own importance and needs and wants aside in service of birdsong? Perhaps.

Baby Schema is a very funny and very serious collection. Galleymore's craft is assured and her lines of approach wonderfully surprising and fresh. The apparent simplicity and readability of her poems belies how clever they are. Ecopoetry of personal responsibility in the face of biological imperative – yes please!

About the Author
Angela Cleland is a poet, novelist, teacher and audio narrator. Her most recent collection is *Real Cute Danger* (Broken Sleep, 2022).

BELINDA COOKE

Peter Sirr, *The Swerve*, 97pp, Gallery Press

Harry Clifton, *Gone Self Storm*, 94pp. Bloodaxe Books

Peter Sirr's individuals in *The Swerve*, though insignificant in the vastness of history's perennial conflicts, can still 'remain untiringly alive' (Pasternak epigraph to 'Lines for My Daughter'), each of us unique in our own particular moment: 'There's a kind of secret knowledge / enfolds us, reaches everything we do, ... // ... the universe is waiting, / patient and inexhaustible.' ('A Saxon Primer') And, for Sirr personally, this 'secret knowledge', ranges through philosophy, language, ancient and contemporary warfare, AI, Buson, Borges and the Tang poets, varying in tone from the elegiac to the humorous, thought-provoking and heartbreaking all at the same time.

Sirr's trademark has always been to hint at the transcendental in our ordinary lives and settings:

... Most of what goes on
goes like the shadows across walls
unseen, the world shines beyond us.
Somewhere a treasure is clasped in a dying hand
and the things go on in their own lives,
... .
            ... the day that will gather
everything waiting, everyone lost, and join them
together again.'
   ('Light in June')

The smallest thing triggers it: 'Something / some shaft of sun or bird cry', that recalls his mother, where it is as if '... the trees, the lilies bright on the lake, / the small rain on the water might know / it is your birthday again today.' ('23.6.20') While in 'May' dead poets' language remains ever alive in nature: '... drenched in finches, rooks, blackbirds, / each of whose songs will have lines of yours, / as the trees and sky will have your soul'.

Similarly, he uses the most everyday word in

Sirr's trademark has always been to hint at the transcendental in our ordinary lives and settings ...

unexpected ways to map our lives. In 'Meanwhile', 'It's that nothing happens afterwards / or everything happens all the time':

> You're gone but: meanwhile your car reverses out
> and a new life parks in the drive.
> Meanwhile is where you live now
> watching the clouds go by.'

While 'The Swerve's' hurtling momentum shows a chance skid has him '... swerved out of time and the clear road' to journey back to his grandparents' home, and 'a life more crowded, generous', only to bring the reader up short with the brute fact of his father's neurological illness, and a return to inform the family: '... this is why we've come, / this is the swerve tilts him off his course':

> ... it's for
> everything that moved from saying, for the
>   forgotten playing,
> the whole unspoken ceremony, and the seconds
>
> when the swerving briefly halted, became a holding.

But it is history's brutality that takes centre-stage to the individual's walk-on part, leaving us unsurprised at 'A Valediction' 's parting shot: 'Goodbye, year, we thought / you'd never leave.' Sirr takes us from history's dawn, to its science-driven, post-apocalyptic conclusion, seemingly resigned to the perennial cycling of swords and ploughshares: 'One god is born. Another dies' ('A Birth in Winter'), while 'River' suggests history's Heraclitian flux and its tools to create and destroy: 'The tools accompany us, speak for us, / whatever we do flows on'. The unrelenting war images are timeless, but currently all too familiar, with Ukraine and Gaza on our screens: 'A man moves through the rubble foraging for rainwater. // When everything is gone the cursing begins.' ('Salt'); 'The fires burn, you won't see home again // and always someone is standing beyond consoling, / his butchered children in the rubble and mud.' ('Reading the Tang Poets'). Similarly pertinent is 'Steps' where he points to why people remain in their bombed-out houses:

> History is a nervous conversation
> over stale bread and hard-won water,
> the holding of hands and the comfort of love
> through dark nights lit by fear.
> History is eleven floors in the target zone
> where quiet footsteps go up and down.

Along with such directness, Sirr is also endlessly inventive in his shifts of tone. Dark comedy and tragedy go hand in hand. In the intriguing 'Border Control', his entertainingly demotic juxtaposes integrity with compromising to survive in a world turmoil, where holding on to our identity is struggle enough:

> Not everything I said I did
> I did in fact. Not literally.
> But if it wasn't all true,
> it was tru-ish.

He then proceeds with the amusing comparison of angels taking backhanders to let the imperfect into heaven:

> You think they're all
> kosher? No angel
> ever looked the other way?

But the collection's absolute gem is 'Haunting School' which sits well with his poems on a post-apocalyptic nowhere. The speaker's initial bliss at the liberation of becoming a ghost, moves on to poltergeist-like tantrums at the human absence, until the final realization that this is it forever, loss of place, self, and loved ones: 'the empty earth is your forever workplace'.

The Swerve is a skillfully crafted collection where stand-alone poems feed into the collection's numerous interconnected seams. Sirr brings the whole tour de force to an uplifting conclusion as it moves into the new

But it is history's brutality that takes centre-stage to the individual's walk-on part ...

year, though it is hard to know where his hope is going to come from as he invokes in 'Breath' Jerusalem's metaphorical significance as a place of peace:

Jerusalem drift among us
walk the narrow streets beside us
let your cool breath greet us
wherever we turn.

The diaspora Irish may talk warmly of 'going home', but for **Harry Clifton** in *Gone Self Storm* it is hard to define – 'Aching Void' could have been the title poem. Conceived on his parents' departing ship he sails: '... north, out of waters / I never cease to explore' ('A Ship Came from Valparaiso'), while 'Chile' prepares us for the unknown 'void' of his mother's impoverished past:

... I have yet to be born,
To come into the knowledge of myself and
go back home

To the locus of pure suffering, before history,
Picking up baggage along the runway,

Keeping the orphan in me loved, and the salt-
mine worker fed,
Claiming as birthright, all that was left unsaid.
('Chile')

The first section takes us into the heart of that suffering, but as he shifts to Ireland, don't expect *Macbeth's* porter to pop in for light relief, but a flurry of elegies to family and many artist friends. The silver lining is the poetry he writes as a result. Rootlessness and a lifetime of travel, gives him a unique take on self and landscape, while language, though one of '... conditionals, subjunctives / In a land of might-have-been' ('Chile'), has enabled him to learn 'the true home of the poet is not in a place but in the language itself,' ('Biography'). This all makes for some great, seriously sad writing, all expressed in a classy, deceptively effortless, limpid style.

His Chilean mother's impoverished childhood and difficulty adapting to Ireland has left its mark on Clifton. In *The Irish Times* (5/03/23) he calls his work 'the poetry of unlove' due to a family rift with his maternal grandmother: '... she had become my first and only muse, the muse of the absent female, unloved, unloving, giving the lie to family, in touch with another life'. Clifton conveys all this loss with the following simple image:

I come up behind them
Gently now, and take her
By the waist, and feel it,
Their silent weeping

All of them, as the heads,
The hair scraped back
For daily duty, lean against me
In their lonely millions.
('Woman's Home Companion')

Note how the child, in role reversal, tries to comfort the adults with a futile gesture which captures both the excluded child and Clifton the adult absorbing their grief into his fingers, for look close and one sees it is not an actual memory but an imagined action – the 'gently now' suggesting it's only now that he can forgive the loss it was to him as a child.

This 'Unlove' then travels down the family. Born out of Chile's poverty and an Irish ex-Pat workforce, first we have his grandparents: 'Void on void, as man as wife, / To married bliss, an afterlife / Of haunted sons and daughters.' ('To the Engineer Herbert Ashe'), and then his similarly doomed parents:

A desert behind her, alcohol, orphanhood.
You explain to her about history, about home.
She tells you about emptiness, the void.
She will stand for your anthem.
('Sin-eater')

This leaves Clifton – the 'sin-eater' – left, 'to feast on both your love-letters, / Share your grave, like an expiated ghost'. Later he is one of the few visitors to

Rootlessness and a lifetime of travel, gives him a unique take on self and landscape, while language ...

the estranged grandmother in her bed-sit – note here how he conflates the literal and metaphorical: '[looking] In her garden of long grass, her junkyard of Eden, / For a lever, a latch-key, some way in / To the first address, and the shame of origin' ('The Widow Transitito'). He subsequently casts himself as the 'stepchild' or 'orphan', but now with his adult understanding of why his mother was unable to love him as he needed:

> That I was motherless
> No one told me. That your emptiness
> Was holy, a lifetime in the desert,
> I would find out for myself.
>   ('Stepmother')

These dysfunctional family poems are certainly the most harrowing, but space allows one to only touch on the rich trove of poetry that follows them as he ranges through life in Dublin, travels around Kerry, and on to his wife the novelist Deirdre Madden's family home in Antrim, as well as ranging across landscapes he has known from their years living away. Ultimately, landscape becomes something internalized:

> And the blue-green waters, the constellations
> After dark, the wrecker's moon and the tides
> Are all inside me, who was put ashore
> To walk this way, before and after Ireland.
>   ('On Ventry Sand')

Death dominates with elegies to so many important people from his past. As he visits Dublin's Glasnevin Cemetery, famed for many notable figures, he looks for his father's side. Though, ostensibly, he has more to go on, he has to separate fact from heroic myth. Here, we have Margaret Doran who took part in the Irish Civil War against the Free State, and, along with it, the inevitable meditations on one's own mortality:

> Whose city went up in flames,
> Who vanishes, with the other names.
> As I do, as I will,

> Bitter knowledge, bitter pill,

> Filling in time, Glasnevin clay,
> Between now and death,

> tomorrow and yesterday,
> Tidying up the myth.
>   ('Glasnevin Clay 3. Margaret Doran 1893-1983)

The pleasure and challenge of writing a review on Harry Clifton's poetry is that every poem gives you a multi-layered journey of its own. One superb example of this is the sequence 'The Felling'. Read it a hundred times and it will give you an added layer. The felling of a group of pines provides an extended metaphor for those who had sheltered beneath their branches: '... Arcadian grove / Once picnicked in by sisters, maiden aunts // Now shades of themselves'. From here he considers that landscape and the whole history of its previous existence along with the physical and psychological impact of their presence and absence, literally, in every sense as he: 'listen[s] for the wind / Yes, but without the trees ... // ... All the sounds that carry / And are lost'. And though I have repeatedly referred to the darkness in his poetry, as we move to the collection's conclusion there is much, like Sirr, that he gains comfort from concluding here, with an encapsulation of life's growth and decay:

> Goodbye dears, and thank you. Everything

> Has run wild again, but nothing is lost.
> I stand in the long grass. Arcadia, Parthenon –
> Everything that shadowed us has gone.

The pleasure and challenge of writing a review on Harry Clifton's poetry is that every poem gives you a multi-layered journey of its own.

About the Author

Belinda Cooke is a Russian translator and poet with seven books to date. Her most recent include a prose memoir on her mother's life: *From the Back of Beyond to Westland Row: A Mayo Woman's Story* (2023) and the poetry collection *With Our Own* (2024) on the diasporic experience, both from The High Windows Press.

IAN McMILLAN

Guillaume Apollinaire translated by Martin Sorrell, *The Bestiary*, £7.20, Arc Poetry

Charlotte Gann, *Cargo*, £9.00, Mariscat Press

Blake Morrison, *Skin and Blister*, £9.00, Mariscat Press

Gill Shaw, *Touching Air*, £6.00, Stewed Rhubarb Press

Emily Oldfield, *Calder*, £7.00, Poetry Salzburg

Elvire Roberts, *North by Northnorth*, £7.00, Five Leaves New Poetry

Jan Norton, *Relief Map*, £7.00, Five Leaves New Poetry

Writers of short stories often say that there's an assumption they're simply a stepping stone on the way to writing The Great Novel of Ideas; stories are apprentice works, foothills leading to the higher mountain of long (maybe too long: discuss) fiction, but of course in the view of many people including me the literary short story is its one form and it doesn't need the novel to aspire to.

The same is often said of pamphlets, that a pamphlet is the waiting room before the door opens to the glittering palace of the full collection but I like pamphlets as pamphlets rather than calling cards or visions of the future, and here's a fine crop of recent ones.

Arc Poetry in Todmorden have been publishing beautifully-produced new work for decades, but in this fantastic translation of one of the fathers of surrealism, **Guillaume Apollinaire**'s 1911 collection *The Bestiary*, takes us right back to the fountainhead of so much writing that's being produced today. Apollinaire seems, like Debussy, effortlessly modern with his playfulness, his subverting of structure, his freedom to experiment with tradition. Bestiaries have a long tradition, going back at least as far as Medieval times; they're stories of real and mythical animals that often have a moral attached to them and Apollinaire delightfully subverts this tradition in tightly-organised poems of mostly four lines. Here's 'The Dolphin':

Dolphin, you play among the waves
Yet how bitter stays the sea.
So what if now and then my joy erupts?
Life keeps up its cruelty.

Martin Sorrell, the translator, in helpful notes above the poem, tells us that 'the implication is that, just as the friendly dolphin is betrayed by the sea – in the form presumably of its human predators – so the joyful poet is all too easily swallowed up by malicious forces'. He's right and all! I like the dual-language presentation of the pamphlet, too, tempting armchair translators like me to have a go, and why not?

Mariscat Press, like, Arc, have been bringing out vital work for a long time, and there are two shining examples here. In *Cargo* **Charlotte Gann** gives us glimpses into a life that becomes, like all our lives, unique and universal. The pamphlet reminds me that poetry is one of the best ways that humans have of talking to each other with honesty in whatever poetic form the language takes. Imagine these poems as clothes hung out to dry; imagine the reader as the breeze, drying them until they're ready to wear. 'Two Lamps' is a very good example of a poem of unrequited love, set in that contemporary arena of desire, the office.

Across the gulf of darkness I can see
your light on, too. The hunch of your self
over your desk, through two hatches.

And later in the same poem:

The whole floor is silent.
Will you come across and say goodnight
this evening. Why don't I leave?

I really like the erotic tension of the poem, the isolating obsession of 'your self', and the mock-inclusion of 'your light on, too.' Look: both our lights are on!

In 'Calling Time' Gann gives us a description of a night out that, maybe featuring the same people from 'Two Lamps', spirals out of control:

> *Apollinaire seems, like Debussy, effortlessly modern with his playfulness, his subverting of structure, his freedom to experiment with tradition.*

and they're calling a warning
and stacking chairs at the other end of the
    narrow room
and we're the only table left and still

we are drinking and shouting

And maybe that's old Apollinaire in the corner.

The poet and novelist **Blake Morrison**, in his Mariscat Press pamphlet *Skin and Blister*, has written a moving elegy to his sister Gillian. The tight forms, (sonnets and a sestina) allow Morrison to build deep emotion from craft and art so that the poems become love letters to loss:

I left and
spent three years at uni; you stayed behind.
But here we are, something between us still.
tete-a-tete in the middle of a party,
your eyes so bright their light can never die.

The poet is always present, as brother and writer, and towards the end of the sequence the writing becomes almost unbearably emotional, the tears breaking through Morrison's control, for the one reading and the one writing:

Two years to the day, I'm sitting in the spot
where the news came through, under skies
    you'd kill for,
primed to go – pen, notebook, cafetiere-
but failing to compose a final sonnet

and later in the same poem, the dead sister speaking and the poet replying:

I want to get on with oblivion.
You can't keep writing my obituary.
Slipping off behind cloud, the sun just went out
(and the sonnet I've not written is complete).

And, like the Apollinaire made me want to try my hand at translation, *Skin and Blister* encourages me to have a go at a sestina. That's tonight's task.

Touching Air by **Gill Shaw**, published by Scotland's Stewed Rhubarb Press, is a viscerally vivid hymn of praise to queer love and loss and the body's centrality to the mind's obsessions and wanderings:

take your forefinger
trace the lines of my tattoos
remind me to breathe
  ('Senryu for Luna')

Shaw is very good at the power of the list as a taxonomy of emotion, as in '15 Ways To Stay Alive':

1. Cry. As often as you need to, so you don't drown
    from the inside.
2. Cast a binding spell to undo her magic.
3. Make an appointment for acupuncture. Let the
    acupuncturist read heartbreak on your tongue

And in 'The things that I am left with' she makes the quotidian resonate with meaning:

Theatre tickets. A tin of paint. Insomnia. The last drops in a department store sample of your favourite perfume. A print of the moon as it looked overhead on the night that we met.

This pamphlet is so good at reminding us that the so-called ordinary can be a portal into the extraordinary, and that words are the footprints of being alive.

Emily Oldfield, in *Calder* takes us on a journey through those parts of Yorkshire that seem to brim and seethe with magic. She gives these West Yorkshire locations a shamanic presence that lingers at the unexplored edge of the map. The language ties itself to the location:

Here *Dean, Clough, Royd*
seeded deep in the chest
the rough of local tongue

The poet is always present, as brother and writer, and towards the end of the sequence the writing becomes almost unbearably emotional ...

in this wood-panelled throat
('Ramsden')

and explores the land's effect on the body:

The foot knows
and hand follows,
the contours' calligraphy steers
the pen
('Basin Stone').

Emily Oldfield is very good at handling the poem's building block, the phrase: 'contours' calligraphy' and 'this wood-panelled throat' in these examples, and elsewhere 'the flood of your secret' and 'shrapnel of vowels.' These phrases build into a kind of language-music that drives the poems until they become psalms of praise and warning for a part of the country that is always available for myth.

Five Leaves in Nottingham is a splendid independent bookshop that I'd recommend you visit next time you're round those parts, and I'm pleased to announce that they've revived their publishing arm with a selection of fine pamphlets celebrating new voices. Maybe more independent bookshops should do this; they're already creative literary hubs, so why not take that extra step? I know it's easier said than done, mind you, but it might be worth a try.

Jan Norton's *Relief Map* is a beautifully-articulated autobiography in verse. Here are gleaming snapshots of a life in an allotment,

Beyond her rose bed, he heaves rhubarb
out of baked sod, pink into the daylight
('Cultivation')

In arguments and abuse heard from next door
we listen to muffled hatred through the wall
till silence, cold as Sundays, settles on the house
('A Kind of Loving')

And the joy of an English teacher, Mrs Savage, allowing young minds to flourish:

Look, she says, pointing to the blackboard
where the words sing sweeter than a blackbird
'*this our life finds tongues in trees.*'
Shakespeare, girls, Shakespeare.

By the end of the pamphlet we feel that we know the poet, and I felt grateful that she'd shared her life with us and I began to wish that more people, whether they see themselves as poets or not, would write down their lives in poems. And in 'Feeling My Age' she seems to have been gazing through my window:

When did I begin to groan on rising
from a soft-cushioned chair, or let out
a sigh before I take a first full gulp of tea?

I'm with you there, Jan!

In *North by Northnorth* **Elvire Roberts** examines the power and powerlessness of language to help us tell our stories. Language is powerful because it articulates meaning and it's powerless because sometimes the meaning that gets articulated isn't quite the one we wanted to articulate but it's as close as we can get, as she says in 'KUN', the opening poem: 'Imagine a sea where imagination outstrips itself.' The pamphlet is packed with visually striking work, the sections of KUN separated by dotted lines and images of scissors, 'Beautiful demoiselle' made up of hexagonal word-containers and 'Concertina' moving down the page in skinny phrases separated by forward and back slashes. The effect isn't gimmicky or showy, though: the poems are enhanced and underlined by these approaches and they take me deeper into the work. *North by Northnorth* is one of the most striking debuts I've read for ages, and I can't wait to read what Elvire Roberts does next.

Pamphlets are vital to the ecology of poetry so don't forget to buy them, read them, subscribe to them if you can. And of course, don't forget to write them.

Five Leaves in Nottingham is a splendid independent bookshop that I'd recommend you visit next time you're round those parts ...

About the Author
Ian McMillan's books include the memoir *My Sand Life, My Pebble Life* (Adlard Coles) and *To Fold the Evening Star: New & Selected Poems* (Carcanet)

JONATHAN DAVIDSON

Robert Selby, *The Kentish Rebellion*, 58pp, £10, Shoestring Press

Helen Tookey, *In the Quaker Hotel*, 110pp, £11.99, Carcanet

Kathryn Simmonds. *Scenes from Life on Earth*, 80pp, 10.99, Salt

David Clarke, *The Field in Winter*, 72pp, 10.99, Nine Arches Press

In **Robert Selby**'s first collection, *The Coming-Down Time*, he signals his interest in an often forgotten corner of the British Isles. While Kent may be marketed as the Garden of England, it is overshadowed by other regions, and the County's resistance during the Civil War is rarely referenced. Selby's building of a whole poetry collection around the Kentish Rebellion of 1648, triggered by Royalist-leaning landowners responding with force to Parliament's rejection of a petition raised in support of the King, is bold.

Selby's approach is both to use the language of modern reporting ("A helmeted / reporter crouches behind a wall, finger to earpiece.") and to present a series of what might be described as 'opinion pieces' or 'features' by and about those caught up in the times. A variety of forms are used, largely metrical and with generous use of epigraphs drawn from contemporary accounts. The latter are vital, and are usefully supplemented by some research on the part of the reader – *The Old Parish of Nonington* website, for instance, offers a good summary.

Most of the first half of the collection is a prelude, offering poems that give insights into the minds of those about to feature in what Alan Everitt, in an epigraph at the start of the book, calls 'the last ... of the great local insurrections of English history.' Selby does well in this section of the book to both release much factual detail, while using empathy and imagination to ensure the reader is entirely immersed. This style of poetry – elegantly phrased, quietly particular in image, immediate but acknowledging the strangeness of those times – is not at all easy to pull off, but here it works.

After a brief Interlude that introduces us to Squire Adam Sprakeling and his turning of a not-uncommon anti-puritanism into serial murder, The Kentish Rebellion itself occupies the last half-of the book. Again, Selby brings into use modern conflict – the lesser and greater mobs who have set upon our towns to incite others, for instance – to whisk the story along. He also offers, for instance, in the fifth poem of this section, a step-by-step guide to musket use:

"With the cartridge in your right hand,
bite off the end
and fill the pan with a little gunpowder;

    close the pan and blow off loose powder,
    making sure to keep the burning match cord
    in your left hand so it doesn't set off
        the charge;"

Wise advice and such that could be found in today's internet if one were so inclined.

It is this sustained interaction with our times that lifts *The Kentish Rebellion* from an account of a little local difficulty to a work that interrogates our own opinions. Selby's dramatis personae are made real with the lightest of touches. Their certainties and uncertainties, their hopes and regrets, the sheer awfulness of warfare in one's own fields, remind the reader that we have much to learn by exploring the past. Any purity of thought or intent is, in one case, "minced by canister shot careering down / from Brockman's two cannon at the top".

Whilst clearly Kent as a County has its peculiarities – what region does not – Selby resists the temptation to present this as a country curiosity. It was small and brief, but it was indicative of those times in the way that a demonstration outside an asylum centre can be indicative of ours. More importantly, Selby convinces that to offer an account of this rebellion through poetry gives as much as many history books and through applied

> *While Kent may be marketed as the Garden of England, it is overshadowed by other regions, and the County's resistance during the Civil War is rarely referenced.*

intelligence transforms our understanding.

In the poem 'Leapfrog' from the section entitled 'Stilled in a Hallway' in Helen Tookey's collection, *In the Quaker Hotel*, a slight but vivid interaction between two young girls is recorded. The matter at issue – how one needs two to play leapfrog – is nicely recorded; amusing, poignant even; but it is the surprising and releasing image in the last of the five stanzas that makes a recollection into a poem:

> Minutes later
> she bursts back out through the French windows,
> begins turning cartwheels the length of the lawn.

These are perfectly turned lines, beautifully aurally balanced (as you'd hope of a description of someone cartwheeling), but they also offer us vicarious wonder.

This coming across a plain moment of wonder – which can be negative as well as positive – is present in many of Tookey's poems, but wherever the poems take us, they are almost always built on a slow, quiet recording of observation. While this might sound like a perfectly obvious thing to say, repeated reading of the poems suggests that the poetry is arrived at *after* the observations have been taken, recorded, examined and considered. In this respect, *In the Quaker Hotel*, is in the increasingly overlooked tradition of poets who 'notice such things' (c.f. Hardy, T. etc.). In 'River Oaks', for instance, a perfectly ordinary (and what a laden phrase that is …) location is quietly subjected to the poet's still gaze. So:

> "The fountain in the memorial garden
> is still in perfect working order
> but the playground is gone."

The language echoes – parodies almost – how we are encouraged to reference civic amenities, with not a word out of place. And it goes on: statements, questions, found quotations, and then finally the narrator – let us say the poet, for it is probably she – looking hopefully into a little pond to see, what? To see fish. But there are no fish, instead:

> Sunlight dazzles,

> flashes off the surface like a signal off a mirror,
> a message sent across some vast distance.
> Much too late by the time you receive it.

How important it is in this poem, to wait and wait and wait and then offer that final line that opens up the whole poem. It looks easy, I suspect it isn't.

The poems mentioned so far have forms which hardly draw attention to themselves, as befits their methods. In other pieces, Tookey wades into slightly less common forms. In 'Pool/Other Body' the right justified lines of the poem are reflected onto the opposite page, with all words visible in reverse order but at least half almost disappeared in faint type. This poem offers several ways of being read – or perhaps being seen would be the better description. Immediately we are offered a reflection of the dominant, human account the death of some wasps, and then beyond that a widening series of statements about how we see space, what boundaries mean, what being an individual life form might mean. Or so I believe. There's room for alternative views, and that's fine.

Other pieces are composed of sequences of prose, each perhaps containing poetry, but laid out for us to step lightly across, building a sense of narrative but also forming an impressionistic whole. While these are interesting, absorbing, enjoyable journeys, the poems in *In the Quaker Hotel* for this reviewer work best when they compress themselves into a straight-edged form – the three line stanzas, the couplets, the dozen or so lines only. Restraint within constraints releases the poetry, or so so many of these poems suggest. Hard, this, to capture in short quotes, but here are the last lines of 'Eighteen', just such a poem:

> you pose for a picture
> arms outflung   as though to say
> all this –   so much –

How important it is in this poem, to wait and wait and wait and then offer that final line that opens up the whole poem. It looks easy, I suspect it isn't.

smile awry   as though to say
what is it you are leaving me –

Frighteningly painful that last line, for this reader. The poem 'The Doll's House', from **Kathryn Simmonds**' collection *Scenes from Life on Earth*, manages to be witty, funny and poignant. The premise is simple: describe a doll's house in a state of having been well played with by whichever child owns it and let the incongruousness of 'Daddy fully clothed and showering' and 'big sister at her computer, / orange wool hair flying straight up to the sky' and then leave us with:

And Mummy lies on her hard bed
in the middle of the afternoon,
dreaming with her eyes open.

Ibsen was less succinct (and lighter on laughs).

Exploiting the otherness of the ordinary threads itself through so many of Simmonds' poems, making them deliciously easy to read and quietly subversive. As with Helen Tookey, noticing things seems to be the starting point; looking beyond one's self, even looking beyond humanity and – let's say it – applying some imagination. In 'Moths' we are offered both a richly imaginative series of descriptions of moths in their various forms, including that of carrier of human dreams:

poured in from back gardens
or abandoned dreams,   flotsam,
pieces of ourselves   returned
in air,
eyelids snipped from the dead
& made to fly,
   ('Moths')

That ampersand is rather good, conveying the right degree of matter of fact-ness but drawing the eye to the sense of what it is persuading us. And despite what I said earlier, about Symmonds thinking beyond humanity, the moths in this poem have an uncanny knack of knocking us for six with their quiet associations with all our troubles. So, I would do better to suggest that so many of the poems in *Scenes from Life on Earth* look out at the world in order to look in on ourselves. A simple – deceptively simple – example is the poem 'Snow', quoted in its entirety:

In these startling deep drifts
I think of them
a hundred miles away
beneath fresh quilts of snow,
together / not together,
body beside body, like us,
not touching as we sleep.

And a special mention for her poem 'Unequal Love', which although it is in a long line of poems about children being breezily unaware of how their parents love them, manages to be genuinely moving, quotable, sharable, the real thing.

I do like that the opening poem in David Clarke's third collection, 'Reciting a Poem by Czeslaw Milosz at Krasnogruda', suggests that the poems in *The Field in Winter* will mesh with a world of literature beyond our island shores. Remarkably, this opening poem offers us the poet amongst some Polish villagers, reciting poetry. It ain't the chuffing Archers. Good. And better, that in this poem and in all his poems, Clarke uses a slow, steady beat to understand what is observed. In the speaking of the poem, he observes:

The villagers listen politely as I stumble
over the poem's uneven threshold –
If I could at last tell you what is in me.
These words turn for a moment in my mind
before the tongue can catch them, briefly,
on their flight through birch and thicket,
to ignite the lake's dark eye.

There is a quizzical ruefulness, reflective but not obsessive, careful, honest. A poem that might have lent itself to whimsical self-study, in Clarke's hands is

> *Exploiting the otherness of the ordinary threads itself through so many of Simmonds' poems, making them deliciously easy to read and quietly subversive.*

always alert to the incongrousness of the reality of our situation. In 'Fen Lane' we are offered:

> Here cider drinkers make their dens
> in hollows of coat-ripping thicket.
> A pink sock flaps in razor wire
> around a substation's hum.

In this poem, as in many, there is a tension, between our inclination to seek release and purification from the natural world and the reality which requires us to acknowledge the 'fly-tipped mattresses', etc. This tension is accentuated by the seeming formality of the poems, all of them, each presented neatly with a stanza of some form, reminding us that from constraint of expression comes freedom of thought.

This use of form also reminds us that these are not the first poems to be written by an observant poet about the natural – or sometimes unnatural – world around them, and if we are to be reminded of Hardy and Housman and Edward Thomas, that is no bad thing. So, should we be concerned about the use of the rather unfashionable word 'slough' in the line 'It sloughs off all coordinates' in the poem 'Cherry Blossom', or even that this is a poem about cherry blossom? No. It works, and that the subject of this poem echoes previous poems by at least one of the aforementioned, simply adds to the richness of not only reading the poem but – wake up at the back – thinking about the poem.

Reading and re-reading – and speaking aloud, quietly – the poems in *The Field in Winter*, is an act of immersion in a broadly flowing river of poetry. It pays to read around, to chase off across that field in whatever season and gather a few more poems about cherry blossoms or starlings or storks or foxes to see how wonderfully Clarke's poems not only speak for themselves but link arms with their fellow poems. There is not a poem here that will not reward a little bit of enquiry, which is the highest praise I can offer for a very fine collection.

About the Author

Jonathan Davidson's books include *Downland* (Two Rivers Press) and *A Commonplace* (Smith|Doorstop)

EDMUND PRESTWICH

Kit Fan, *The Ink Cloud Reader*, 96pp, £11.69, Carcanet Poetry

Hasan Alizadeh (translated and introduced by Kayvan Tahmasebian and Rebecca Ruth Gould), *House Arrest*, 60pp, £10.99, Arc Publications

The Ink Cloud Reader is prefaced by an anecdote which imagines a famous Fourth Century AD Chinese calligrapher as a student trying to 'read' the clouds of ink in the pond in which he's made to wash his brush. So the title suggests both the book's difficulty and its concern with finding meaning and creating beauty in the teeth of the world's confusion and violence and the inevitability of death. Difficulty comes both from its forms and the nature of its content: straddling public and private experience, it presents both in fragmentary terms and the latter in oblique and reticent ones as well. For the right reader it's an impressively skilful, dazzlingly inventive and sometimes moving book that speaks strongly to the confusions of contemporary life.

The first poem, 'Cumulonimbus', develops from the idea that the calligrapher might 'read' cumulonimbus clouds in the inky pond. Moving easily in terms of syntax and metre, it's full of quiet redirections that make its tone and overall bearing elusive. It begins

> Halfway through my life
> the reeds by Meguro River
> where the ducks made love
> stop whistling. I fear I've over-
> inked, or the linseed oil
> soured the sky. The wind
> tastes of oysters grilled
> over autumn soil.

Allusions both enrich this and set the reader's

For the right reader it's an impressively skilful, dazzlingly inventive and sometimes moving book that speaks strongly to the confusions of contemporary life.

compass spinning. It crosses worlds in geography and time – Trecento Tuscany and modern Japan. Echoing the opening of Dante's *Commedia*, the first line absorbs that work's epic, public resonance but in replacing Dante's '*our* life' with '*my* life' Fan steps back from the representative to the individual. The next two lines have an intimately personal air: the speaker's imagination seems to linger over a memory whose significance he doesn't share. References to over-inking and linseed oil link back to the calligraphy school of the preface and suggest the idea of the poet worrying about the success of his compositions. Metaphor becomes abstract, even surreal in 'the linseed oil / soured the sky' but the following lines bring a breeze of sensuous immediacy. Oblique and elliptical as this is, I think it works beautifully, partly because the phrasing is so precisely evocative, partly because the poet's reticence invites the reader to collaborate in the imagining of scenarios and the creation of meanings more than he or she would if the poet gave more definite or consistent guidance. This gives the poem a less circumscribed suggestiveness than poetry of ready self-disclosure can have.

Many of the poems are experimental in form. 'Suddenly' starts with an epigraph from Elmore Leonard, 'Never use 'suddenly', the most over-used, least-needed word in fiction' and consists of a series of very short prose paragraphs all including the word 'suddenly'. The following two-page spread, called 'Delphi', is made up of nine very thin columns, each beginning with an explosively capitalized 'IF' and consisting of a series of questions. Poem after poem, in fact, takes a radically different form. All Fan's formal inventions seemed to me to have a clear expressive value in relation to their poems' particular material. However, what I personally most enjoyed was the way lines of lyrical simplicity and poignancy were highlighted and gained depth of meaning by suddenly emerging from the perplexed matrix surrounding them.

Ink Cloud Reader gains depth and imaginative reach from the way many of its poems are saturated in allusions to literature from different cultures, moving kaleidoscopically between them and the different places in which the author has lived in fact or in mind. 'Year of the Rat', for example, starts with a quotation from Frost's 'Birches' – 'Earth's the right place for love' – only to flee to

> another middle-aged
> galaxy – rocky, aqueous, Earth-sized
> but not Earth-bound – where indigo flamingos
> make alpine nests the shape of globe artichokes

When the poem returns to Earth and to a birch tree (not in Frost's New England forest but in some urban setting with concrete steps) it does so via reflections drawing together Odysseus, Persephone, the poet's partner, Japanese knotweed and sakura (cherry blossom, celebrated in Japan as symbolising hope on the one hand, transience on the other). The end note bleakly juxtaposes reference to 'an off-white image of eroded flesh and failure' with a final italicised quotation from Frost's poem, '*I don't know where it's likely to go better*'.

The penultimate poem, 'Epidaurus', is similarly allusive. Epidaurus itself is the site of a famous ancient Greek theatre and of the temple of the healer god Asclepius. Connecting the classical Greek world and that of the Chinese calligrapher, the poet imagines ink flooding through the sockets of his eyes while he waits for Asclepius. The 'lost people of / Yemen and Rakhine' bring to mind the 'Lost people of Treblinka and Pompeii' of Derek Mahon's 'A Disused Shed in Co. Wexford'. However, against the bleakness of 'Year of the Rat', 'Epidaurus' embraces transience in a spirit of desperate, determined affirmation, clashing images of beauty against those of destruction and atrocity:

> as if the sun, the sight of sea squills, the scent of pine,
>   wild sage and oregano
> alone could heal
>
> our first and last loves, the shattered ice, burning hills,
>   lost people of
> Yemen and Rakhine –

All Fan's formal inventions seemed to me to have a clear expressive value in relation to their poems' particular material.

> but I'm wading in, catching the spring water with
> my mouth,
> and taking my share of every single moment.

The strenuousness with which this poem moves between high-cultural allusions and simple lyricism is itself a moving reflection of divisions within this Hong Kong born poet who in this poem dreams of himself as playing 'all the Odysseuses yet to be translated / arguing with himselves' (sic).

The poems in **Hasan Alizadeh**'s *House Arrest* are translated and introduced by Kayvan Tahmasebian and Rebecca Ruth Gould. What I got out of them was above all streams of vivid and expressive images. Like Fan, Alizadeh weaves together strands from different cultural traditions. Some of his poems relate to Iranian public life, some to the Old and New Testaments or Greek and Roman mythology, some apparently to the personal experience of the poet himself. The introduction tells us that he started as a short story writer. His poems usually do involve story but their fundamental impulse is lyrical. Taking the overall narrative arc for granted, they tend to present one moment within it in an extremely vivid way, suggesting an emotion or complex of emotions. This is true even of a poem like 'Feuilleton'. It begins with something that as well as being a startling image looks like an intriguing narrative hook:

> I fell in love with a sweet-lipped
> bitter-eyed
> girl from Balkh.

Not much develops from this hook, however. We're told, in a summary way, what went wrong with the relationship: the poet delighted in the girl's 'body whiter than jasmine' and her 'flower-scented lips', but was too young and careless to be interested in her mind:

> I had nothing to do with her strange
> sweet & bitter girlish dreams.

To me it's disappointing that her sweetness and bitterness are simply repeated, taken as given, not explored imaginatively. There's a kind of flatness there. The poem ends with the speaker's haunting sense of loss, expressed in a sad cadence reminiscent of the end of some of Ezra Pound's Cathay poems – 'I sigh and sigh'. However, what 'Feuilleton' doesn't have is the compelling, intricately dynamic narrative life of a poem like Pound's 'Exile's Letter' as it evolves towards its wistful conclusion.

Sometimes the images of these poems are anchored in literal-seeming scenarios and sometimes, as in 'Old Testament, New Testament', they're of a more fantastical kind, dissolving and reforming like pictures in a dream. Some work as momentarily living, camera flash glimpses into imagined situations. Some have a wider but more indefinite resonance, like the beautiful single line 'The silence of the sirens' songs' forming the final section of 'Margins', six micropoems about Ulysses' return. Most of the poems in this book work very well on this imagistic level. Admittedly they sometimes fail to come as fully alive as wholes as the vitality of individual phrases suggests they should. Whatever may be the case in the original, in translation these less successful poems seem to me to lack expressive life in their rhythms and syntax. Fortunately, and it's to the translators' credit that this should be so, there are others in which parts and even whole poems do achieve rhythmical beauty and expressiveness.

A fundamental similarity between Alizadeh's and Fan's books is that they both reflect the tensions and interweaving of cultures that is such a feature of the twentieth and twenty-first century world. In this way, they both bring challenging and widening perspectives to the reader's grasp of the world. A fundamental difference, however, is in the fact that Alizadeh's poems are translated and Fan's are not. Another is that where Alizadeh seems essentially a lyrical poet, Fan is a much more conceptual figure who, for all the beauty of his touches of lyricism, explicitly presents himself as wrestling with ideas, and in doing so draws the reader into sharing the evolution of those ideas within and between the poems.

Like Fan, Alizadeh weaves together strands from different cultural traditions.

About the Author

Edmund Prestwich lives in Manchester and taught for many years at the Manchester Grammar School. He is the author of two collections and reviews poetry for several magazines.

JAMES CARUTH

Mark Roper, *Beyond Stillness*, 86pp, €12.50, The Dedalus Press

Jane Clarke, *A Change in the Air*, 74pp, £10.99, Bloodaxe Books

Gillian Clarke, *The Silence*, 80pp, £11.69, Carcanet

These three poets are attuned to the landscape that surrounds them and to nature, its animals, birds and insects. From that viewpoint they look outwards to the wider world. In this I am reminded of how Patrick Kavanagh saw the epic in the ordinary. A way of being rooted in a place and looking outwards, translating events into a personal tongue.

Mark Roper is an English poet who has lived in Ireland for the last forty-four years. His poetry is a celebration of nature and the rural landscape that surrounds him. He is an acute observer of the countryside and our place in it; its birds and animals, the harmony of the natural world, all of it tied to the seasons.

The poems are never complacent but rather there is a sense of urgency, a recognition of our failure to protect our environment and in the later poems, a realisation of the poet's own mortality:

> how soon we get used to it,
> the ground under our feet, going.

He manages throughout the collection to maintain a sense of calm, a quiet intensity through listening to what the world is telling him, a tendency to pause at the end of many of the poems, giving the words time to settle so they permeate our senses:

> we sat on in the dark, listening
> to warmth leaving the stones in the wall,
> hearing acorns falling five fields away.

Like Michael Longley, his poetry has a close affinity with the myriad of birds and wild plants that share his landscape, each one claiming a place, a meaning within the poems, though never with any hint of sentimentality. They are witnesses to the damage we have caused to our environment though in the end they remain survivors:

> To hear again that slow, sad jubilation,
> To see the miles let go of each wing,
> to feel the breath of wild they bring
> to these damp fields.
> ....
> To know this still happens. To know
> they will be here tomorrow and tomorrow.

In his poem 'Coum Éaga' he slips in a declaration, easing its effect with a line break and following it immediately with an almost nonchalant comment about birds, as if the approach of death is something to be taken in his stride:

> I came here when told I hadn't long
> to live. The wheatears I saw then are not
> the ones I see now. In Death Coum,
> what survives? What survives is Spring.

The later poems include a number referencing treatment for cancer and one specifically addressed to Saint Peregrine subtitled *Patron saint of those suffering from cancer* where he speaks without any degree of self-pity

> Filled as I am
> not with rejoicing
> but rapid, aggressive growth

These are courageous poems, from a poet who revels in the world around him, a world that will continue from one season to the next:

> Between them
> cello and bird do what great art
> has been said to do – harmonize
> the sadness of the universe.

Like Michael Longley, his poetry has a close affinity with the myriad of birds and wild plants that share his landscape, each one claiming a place ...

Jane Clarke's third full length collection *A Change in the Air* has already collected a short-listing for the T S, Eliot Prize 2024. Her poems are rooted in the world she inhabits – an Irish rural childhood on a farm in Roscommon to her present home in Glenmalure, Co Wicklow. They are rich with the austerity of her childhood, the influences of her family, the loss of her father and her mother's failing memory and subsequent death. Moving on to the present, her new life in Co Wicklow and marriage, away from the harsh expectations of farming.

Throughout these poems we see her close connection with the natural world, the birds and animals that accompanied daily life in her childhood; her intimate interaction with the landscape and people around her. Her keen eye is constant throughout.

The collection is separated into six sequences including *All The Way Home* which is a number of poems taken from an illustrated chapbook of that name (Smith|Doorstop, 2019) which was written in response to letters written during the First World War between Albert Auerbach and his sister until his death on 1st September 1918. They are poems of subtle tenderness that speak not only of the love between siblings but of all those others who fought and those who waited.

She is a poet of great skill, her language is shaped and eloquent, emotional but totally without sentimentality. At times the simplicity of her words and her frequent choice of the couplet form might suggest an ease that deeper reading of these poems will soon dispel.

In the opening sequence of her childhood and growing up on a farm in Roscommon, she shows a tender picture of her mother after the death of her father, who has had to take over the duties of running a farm, tending to the livestock and bringing up a child amongst poverty and austerity.

This was an Ireland where women in the main, were there to support the man of the house, to carry out their duties and keep silent. These poems look behind this preconception and unearth the love that existed within her parents' marriage:

Every day without him
Is too long;

she's waiting
with the tired cows at the gate.

Her language is exact in depicting their day-to-day existence, the hardness of lives lived under such circumstances, yet every line is watermarked with love and tenderness. Where even the family dog contributes a loving example:

till near the end

when his legs wouldn't carry him
to the back door – long after he'd taught us
all he knew about love that waits
in the wind and rain.

These poems contain not only the personal recollections of a woman in growing up, achieving independence and moving on in her life, but include those events with a wider significance to Ireland as a whole – the sequence *You could say it begins* alludes to the effects of the imposition of a border with the six counties in 1921 and the beginning evidence of sectarianism between Catholic and Protestant neighbours in what had previously been close communities:

Next day, neighbours helped them
empty the house and load two carts;
clothes thrown into baskets,
mattresses, blankets, rugs, cups and saucers
wrapped in tea towels, a can of milk,
gifts of cabbage and soda bread.

Sure you'll be back, they said,
when these troubles are settled.

Other sequences relate to a mining disaster in a lead mine in Co Wicklow, the forced eviction and subsequent emigration of tenant farmers in the 19th century and

Throughout these poems we see her close connection with the natural world, the birds and animals that accompanied daily life in her childhood ...

more recently, a wildfire that damaged extensively the landscape in Killarney in 2021.

The final sequence includes a number of poems celebrating her marriage and maintain that unadorned tenderness that permeate her best poems:

> Strange to use this word
> for the woman I love –
> ....
> I practise saying Isobel is my wife
> and it sings to the tune of my life.

These love poems provide a superb finale to the collection that concludes with her invitation:

> Because it's bright till almost midnight
> and the days will be short too soon,
>
> let's stay out here and listen
> for the wood-pigeon's five-note tune.

Gillian Clarke was the National Poet of Wales from 2008 to 2016 and her latest collection *The Silence* begins during lockdown and that sense of isolation can be felt in these poems from the beginning. Time to consider our place in the world and our failure to take care of it:

> Tonight we wake to watch our shadow
> bite the edge, spread, darkening,
>
> till the moon is blood, light lost
> like all we touch, the poles, the oceans,
>
> the wounded wilderness,

She has always been a poet closely in touch with nature, the recurring themes of landscape, weather and the creatures she shares it with. The poems brim with mammals and birds in intimate proximity (in the first seven pages we have fourteen species of birds and animals) as she takes stock of what abundance surrounds her and what is subsequently at risk.

These are powerful poems of a poet pausing during the period of isolation to reconsider man's responsibilities and our failure to face up to climate change and our stewardship of our environment. A world (a Wales) that she compares to the Garden of Eden – "bleeding from / the bite of our first sin". The collection spares no time in letting the reader settle:

> The days have no names.
> The day they count the dead,
> The day they closed the doors,
>   turned off the lights.

but as winter moves into spring there is the first acceptance of hope:

> Hope will come with its mate,
>   with summer, the world in remission.

Her poetry shows such close attention to the world, the landscape of Wales, from which she views events, life continuing in the organised flow of one season into another. She notes the changes wrought by the virus, a new world that "talks, // on line" and where she finds "Each of us alone." A lockdown that due to the isolation of society has also resulted in a reduction in pollution levels:

> the ozone layer clears
> of particulates, of nitrogen dioxide,
> and we breathe again.
>
> In this clean new silence
> all sound is birdsong.

The second half of the collection moves to a series of poems about her mother and her own childhood. There is no distinct separation of the poems as in Jane Clarke's collection, only a subtle change of voice. Here again we can see a sharp eye in her recollection of the past:

> I search memory with only my senses to guide me.

She has always been a poet closely in touch with nature, the recurring themes of landscape, weather and the creatures she shares it with.

Her dress in the landing light, deep blue as the sea
washing over the pebbles as night falls, ink-dark
as twilight over the lake in the darkening park,
....
It goes with her eyes, lapis lazuli, indigo, night.
I'm getting there now.

The bloodline that flows through her is unmistakeably Welsh so she knows well "that secret sense of belonging", which seeps through many of the poems. In the final section of poems her view of the world remains universal, all of us sharing the one space. Yet she knows well how political boundaries can ultimately divide us, set one against another in wars from Bosworth and Flodden to Gaza, Helmund, Aleppo, Mariopol, Kiev:

I slept to the beat of the sea on the shore,

and woke to hear, down wires and radio-waves,
rumours of war,

This is a collection which deserves the reader's full attention. The poems may at times prove uneasy, they will make us think and maybe demand reading again, and again. But they will remain with us.

About the Author

James Caruth's first collection, *A Stone's Throw*, was published by Staple in 2007 and his pamphlet *The Death of Narrative* was the 2012 winner of the International Book & Pamphlet Competition chosen by Carol Ann Duffy. Other publications are *Dark Peak*, (Longbarrow, 2008), *Marking the Lambs* Smith|Doorstop, 2010), *Narrow Water*, (Poetry Salzburg, 2017) and *Speechless at Inch* (Smith|Doorstop, 2021).

SUZANNE CONWAY

Fiona Benson, *Ephemeron*, 117pp, £12, Cape Poetry

John Wedgwood Clarke, *Boy Thing*, 47pp, £8, Arc Publications

Rosie Jackson, *Love Leans over the Table*, 87pp, £10.99, Two Rivers Press

Fiona Benson is a sharp writer unafraid to delve into those uncomfortable, savage places. Her collection *Ephemeron* explores grief, vulnerability, male brutality, fear, desire, shame, disfigurement, and helplessness. She uses the Pasiphaë and Minotaur myth to show how a mother's love is unconditional. This section is helped by the notes at the back explaining the intricate myth, the different interpretations, and Benson's own take on the myth. Benson's Minotaur is viewed with compassion as a child shunned by society who teaches his sister, Ariadne, 'not to be frightened'.

The monstrous King Minos' vengeance in 'Citizens on the Athenian Tribute' shows how the innocent pay for the adults' sins when he 'demands seven daughters / and seven sons every seven years / in reparation for his firstborn's death … // … Seven years' / reprieve; then our children must pay.' Winning the award for the longest poem title: 'Pasiphaë on the Myth that she Cursed her Husband to Ejaculate Scorpions, Centipedes and Serpents if he Made Love to Another Woman' reveals Minos' adultery and warped, insatiable lust: 'his sexual corruption hung about him / like a smell. In his younger days, / all he wanted were young and undeveloped girls …' In 'Minos Hunts Down Daedalus' Minos 'snatches' at Cocalus' daughters' breasts 'with his liver-spotted hands, / gropes the very youngest of them / tries to grab her between her legs … // … [they] bring a bowl of strong Sicilian wine // fortified with poison.' Although the girls reclaim some power here, the message throughout *Ephemeron* is that females, and the vulnerable, are not safe; in 'The Chimp House' a silverback boils over 'like a sudden, lidded pan' and the speaker grabs her daughter and leaves but then reflects: 'isn't this what she must learn – / how if you are female or small, you must run.' In this collection women must be protectors even when rendered helpless, and female strength and dignity somehow win out even amid the shame and submission. In 'Pasiphaë Goes Home' Pasiphaë accepts her failings with the insistent refrain 'call me' but '*call me mother of a deformed child / and I'll tell you there's no such thing –* // *only gentleness, only perfection.*'

In the Insect Love Songs section, Benson's description

In this collection women must be protectors even when rendered helpless ...

is so intricate that her research and specialist knowledge is clear. A lot of the poems are highly charged, sexualised and give the graphic details. In 'Mama Cockroach, I Love You', the mother's love knows no bounds: 'then feed your pale brood / secretions from your anus ... // ... Because you would leave your body for your offspring / to dine upon – all the liquors and gravy // of the obscene world ...'

'Firefly Suite', part ii Blue Ghost Firefly is concerned with finding a place of safety:

> It's the rest
> of your life's work
> to make yourself a lid,
>
> a shield, a reinforced roof.
> I too keep guard –
> my daughters
>
> the softest part of me –
> and will die
> at my post.

In 'Firefly Suite' part iii Synchronous Fireflies, a love poem for Benson's husband, James Meredith, the writing is so tender and stunning:

> I'd come so far to see this thing and left you
> alone – but then the dark came down the hill
> at a soft pace, with its quiet spell – like the lull
> between two lovers in a drawn bedroom –
> a thronged darkness into which you might send
> any thought, and find it cupped and held.

In 'Mosquitoes, Mozambique' Benson has compassion for these creatures despite how much harm they may inflict; this description of a female mosquito is seductive: 'filling her soft bulb, dipping her beak for a drop of blood / to ripen her eggs; how her abdomen's rosé flush / deepens to ruby ...' Benson describes the mosquito's bite in all its chilling glory:

> they use two serrated needles
> to cut through your tissues, two needles to
> hold the flesh apart,
> one to insert a chemical spit to keep
> your blood running

Then comes the killer blow – the dead children; the survivors ululate on their way to the 'burial ground'.

'Wasp Theology' is awash with brilliant imagery but the ending falls away into abstraction when it would have been more satisfying to leave the reader with the 'black and yellow flames / ... a thousand simmering tongues'.

Boarding-School Tales takes us back to those events in childhood that are difficult to forget. In 'Red Riding Hood', the matron:

> set us on the dark and haunted landing
> to shiver in our nighties, facing
> the wall, for hours.
> Somewhere in our frightened hearts
> we wait there still.

The nub of the collection comes in 'Queen's Women: Daedalus and Icarus': 'Why can't we leave the story here, our hearts / consoled by the human will to escape the squalor / of our circumstance, to seek a life for our children / in the benevolent elsewhere? // But you already know that something fails.'

John Wedgwood Clarke's collection *Boy Thing* is broken into two sections I Boy thing I-XXXIII made up of thirty-three poems and II Fathers and Sons I-VIII made up of eight poems. Titles for the poems would help orientate the reader at times. A curious fragment opens the collection: 'I made of silence a porcelain bell, / trapped a fly and waited for it to die. // In the gap between bell and sill, / its feet still move, now, then now.' The fly represents the secret the speaker feels he must keep as a young boy; in poem XXIV we learn what the secret is: 'It comes in the post and stinks to high heaven, / the belt from the Mediterranean / heat of his affair ... // I wrap it in a bag and hide it like my

In the Insect Love Songs section, Benson's description is so intricate that her research and specialist knowledge is clear.

cut of a crime ...' The father disappears earlier in poem IX: 'The bedroom blind bright red, my father / enters the room: *look after her* – / then gently closes the door / on his voice.' At a reading of *Boy Thing*, Wedgwood Clarke confirmed writing the collection had helped him to make sense of the past and to find some peace with it; the fragment at the end of the book shows it has been a release: 'Words have made of me a porcelain bell / in the shape of a dancing figure. // I ring it – a slight sound. The fly / knocks twice on the glass and is gone.' When hearing these poems read, I was struck by their tautness and rhythm. In poem II, the reader is transported to the father's shop:

> He lets me count the takings. I build him
> colonnades of silver and copper,
> turn the Queen's head right way up
> on crisp and furry banknotes,
> sellotape the torn, the biro-tattooed
> smelling of sweat and tobacco

'Crisp' and 'furry' refer to some notes being new, others worn, but I questioned whether banknotes were ever furry which took me away from the poem. Irrespective, this is a family struggling to survive financially: 'What we take pours away like the stream ...'

Occasionally the poems are too elliptical in places and pronouns are dropped when they are needed, for instance the beginning of poem I: 'Our shop is known for the home-cooked hams / my father bags with honey and spice, / floats in the blackened sarcophagus ...' I kept reading this and it didn't feel grammatically correct with 'floats' and I felt it needed to read 'they float'.

Wedgwood Clarke grew up in Cornwall and the river Stennack runs through these poems, as does the motif of religion: 'St Ia's chapel'; 'Ark of the Convenant'; 'chapel of pain'; 'I swap my daily prayers / for fishing book and tackle shop' to name a few. 'Hollow' and 'empty', and variations of these words, recur in this collection as the speaker tries to make sense of the father's absence.

The mother is largely absent from this collection which Wedgwood Clarke said was a conscious decision. However, in poem VII her birthday surprise is met with her husband's cruelty: 'She bakes a hazelnut meringue, / a strawberry for each of his years ... // ... She buys me a book and he / throws the book at us. Forty-seven / sharp hard local strawberries. / *Choke on them, why don't you.*'

The Fathers and Sons section left me wanting more. Although the washing line as a 'tree of life' could be more original, Wedgwood Clarke's love for his sons sings in poem VIII:

> The cool white shapes sway and brush against me,
> pegs holding edges and my longing
> for the weight of their bodies on my belly,
> shoulders, knees, as they turn and stream in a flat
> and filling dance, the joy I cannot hold.

I defy any reader not to feel the unbearable ache in this section's opening poem: 'O father weather. O risen wind.' And in the depiction of the speaker with his sons and his father in poem IV: 'They have held my earlobe felts as I held / onto you swaying like a came ... // ... I have no coat equal to your sheepskin's ... // ... It was the last shelter of you I knew ...' In poem V the speaker still has the coat: 'I'll take from it // the last two buttons, amber-grey horn ...' *Boy Thing* is a devastating and wondrous collection that shows how difficult it is to overcome being left; the sense of abandonment runs throughout as does the need for connection. Poem XIX sums it up: 'I don't know how to write / the feeling; how I'm apart with them // looking back at a boy windowed / in a carol of longing ...'

The title of **Rosie Jackson**'s collection *Love Leans over the Table* is adapted from verse nine of the 14th century love lyric 'Blow, Northerne Wind' which she translated:

> Love listened to my every word
> And leaned to me over the table
> And bade me take hold of that treasure
> Of my heart's healing

When hearing these poems read, I was struck by their tautness and rhythm.

As one would expect from a book with this epigraph, many of Jackson's poems are concerned with finding, or celebrating, the balm that heals. In the process she takes us to unusual places and we encounter a German Benedictine abbess in 'Hildegard's Remedy': 'And when a man's mind is buried like coal under the earth, / tie round his head a cloth in which sit cooked grains of wheat. / And let the softened wheat carry to his disheartened mind / memory of warm bread, the comfort of a kitchen where love / holds the ladle'.

The reader is entirely immersed in this world and the writing feels magical. I appreciated the lengthy lines and the 'sit/kitchen' echo but wondered if there was a more satisfying and economical verb than the phrase: 'in which sit'. Towards the end of the poem, the skilful, chilling line break: 'He will pluck a blade ...' leads the reader to believe events could take a sinister turn and we are surprised when it continues: '... of grass taller than his hands, put it to his lips and make it sing.' Jackson is a master of the unexpected.

In 'The Covenant', the speaker visits her father in hospital; this poem has tenderness, humour – with this perfect adjective: 'legs inglorious in traction' – and beautiful description:

> I've just learned to walk.
> And Dad longs to take me in his arms, throw me
> to the ceiling, stroll to Headingley, smell the soot
> of Leeds, lean on a gate to smoke a Woodbine.

'The Night I Grew Old' is concerned with human failing in the aftermath of conceiving a child: '[I] knew without being told / this child would demand of me the impossible, that I / was sliding towards a test I could not pass.'

Jackson's poems are so original that it felt contrived when she chose adapted words from Psalm 22:14 in 'My Father Tries to Make Amends', to conjure her father's voice: *hearken O daughter, I am poured out like water, my heart is like wax.*

With 'Revisiting *The Garden of Earthly Delights* at the Prado' I wanted to stay in the otherworldly realm: 'I lived here once, trapped in this mussel shell' and for it to end on 'Eve's hair weighs more than she does' rather than this reality: 'I used to love Bosch. I put him on the cover of my first book ...'

'Life Shocks' and some other poems announce themselves: 'I'm looking for words to catch strands of fresh willow' which makes the reader aware of the poem as a construct rather than being plunged into its immediacy.

The speaker talks of a shared 'flawed DNA' in 'Talking with My Imaginary Sister', and assumes when a relationship ends in 'Like Jean Shrimpton' that 'I must have let her down'. The speaker is often on the back foot but determined to live the best way she can.

There are many devastating and accomplished poems in this collection, including 'And Would It Have Been Better' where the speaker imagines her son not being born or being born to someone else: 'Better to have / sent him back before his cells rooted too deeply, // back to that pre-formed unsuffering place of stars / and nebulae where souls float like unnamed planets'. This speaker knows the grief of consequence. However, in 'The Golden Bough' there is pain but also a sense of redemption: ' ... I want to cry out, as Frigga did, // to the air and birds and new-found tenderness of the world / that love is surely bigger than grief, than death.'

The reader is entirely immersed in this world and the writing feels magical.

About the Author

Suzanne Conway is a poet, writer and teacher. She has published articles, essays, reviews, and over thirty poems in magazines and anthologies, including *The Poetry Review*, *The Dark Horse*, *The North*, *The Result Is What You See Today: Poems About Running* (Smith|Doorstop), and elsewhere. She teaches for the Poetry School and the University of Exeter.
www.suzanneconway.co.uk

THEOPHILUS KWEK

Momtaza Mehri, *Bad Diaspora Poems*, 128pp, £14.99, Jonathan Cape

Khairani Barokka, *amuk*, 96pp, £12.99, Nine Arches Press

Zaffar Kunial, *England's Green*, 96pp, £12.99, Faber & Faber

Every collection of poems is at some level an exercise in serendipity, given the fluid, not to say scattershot nature of the poet's enterprise. We tap out poems – at our desks, on the train, in the grocery line – and months or years later, if we're lucky, enough looseleaf sheets pile up in the proverbial drawer. In some collections an organising principle emerges naturally, as poems speak to each other in conversation or chorus, though there is always the risk that any internal dialogue escapes the reader. Others are more deliberately set up, with sections that take on stronger personalities on their own. Here the risk can often be greater: that the reader, seeking or perhaps more accustomed to the thrill of happenstance, may fail to be convinced by the shape a book eventually imposes on the poems within it.

Momtaza Mehri's debut collection, *Bad Diaspora Poems*, sets itself an especial challenge. Organised in chronological sections, with clusters of standalone poems that, in places, form loose narrative sequences (for instance, 'You Will Never Tell Your Daughters'–'You Will Deny It All'–'You Will Heave Your Body'), the book shape-shifts easily from the twenty-line staple of creative writing workshops everywhere, to the flowing cadences of a multigenerational epic. Even with the most formally innocuous pieces (like 'Gradations' or 'Apricot Season'), one is never sure if the lines on the page are meant to be read as a self-contained poem, or as part of a longer series unfolding across the rest of the section, the book, or indeed history itself. But that is the joy of this collection, and perhaps part of the point.

The collection opens in the 1830s, introduced by Mehri at the start of the first section as a time when fugitives arriving in the Jubba Valley, Somaliland, formed a 'first wave' of settlers – tough, 'friendless'. Its very first poem turns this adjective on its head, with taut lines framing the parameters within which friendships were struck among these newcomers: 'If we dream in the same language, that makes us friends. / If we flinch from the same hands, that makes us friends' ('Conditionals'). Already, the stories told by this runaway community are steeped in prevarication and myth; one poem, presented as a series of ten commandments, sets down 'A Few Facts We Hesitantly Know To Be Somewhat True', while another's title points tentatively back to '... the Old Country You Have Never Seen'. Amid these shifting certainties, the poet attempts to establish, if she can, what it means to be defined by the scattering force of history – in other words, to find oneself belonging to a diaspora. 'Diaspora is witnessing a murder without getting blood on your shirt', she ventures, before thinking the better of it:

> Of course, there are other definitions.
> Namely, a freshly scraped scalp,
> a dome to your rock, the inevitability of fajr
> and late-night texts.
> Each lie about how good the exchange rate really was.
>   ('Reciprocity is a Two-way Street')

Subsequent sections leap forward by at least a century. First to 1936, marking the violent birth of an Italian colony in the Horn of Africa, then the year of Somali independence in 1960, a new nation arising from the 'scramble for a new story'. These slices of the past are given voice through historical characters adroitly ventriloquised by Mehri, from Mussolini's would-be child assassin, Anteo Zamboni, to the twenty-two poets reading on the last night of the ill-fated International Poetry Festival of 1979 on the Castelporziano beach. But as the sections progress, through several waves of displacement (in 1977, 1987 and again in 1991), to 'Year Zero' (which as one poem hints, is 1990, the year of the poet's own arrival in the UK), Mehri chooses her cast much

'Diaspora is witnessing a murder without getting blood on your shirt', she ventures, before thinking the better of it ...

closer to home – familiar figures discovered, imagined, or lost too soon. Shot through these poems is yearning for a rootedness that was perhaps once experienced by earlier generations, but which the poet herself now only carries as the barest shadow of a memory: 'you wandered your city's tree-lined streets. / Inhaled sharp breathfuls of bougainvillea. / ... / Mother, let me mourn what I have never seen' ('This Little, This Late').

The majority of Mehri's poems are, in essence, declamatory, proceeding in line-length sentences that are primed for the open mic stage: 'No one can tell us where we'll be in a year's time. / We are becoming self-taught in the art of disappearance. / We don't know what we want because we've never had it' ('Balcony Dispatches, 2002'). What saves their oratorical power from being watered down through repetition is the fact that they are skilfully interspersed, at just the right junctures, with a sprinkling of prose poems, erasure poems, and others that demand a different mode of reading. Some formal innovations are perhaps less successful; the liberal use of forward-slashes in 'A Tableau of Aspiration', for instance, does little to vary the rhetorical effect of what are still declamatory sentences, as in:

> ... black poets are big fans
> of rights given / of frothy righteousness / of
> rewriting faithless accounts
> of who we are / of what we can be
> gaseous / with impotent fury / we flail upwards ...

But these are, ultimately, minor quibbles. Mehri knows the best qualities of her writing and deploys them well; it is precisely among these forthright statements and restatements of the diasporic identity as it is lived and breathed – poems that call out 'in praise of all that is honest', to borrow one memorable phrase ('Glory Be to the Gang Gang Gang') – that we gain a sense of how much remains lost, how much remains unnamed.

Moving similarly within this declamatory mode is **Khairani Barokka**'s *amuk*, which begins with the text of a performance lecture sharing the collection's title that was first performed at the University of Edinburgh in 2022. Re-created in book form, this text hovers with precision between affect and argument, borrowing the techniques of the page to approximate what can only be imagined as the compelling cacophony of the original stage performance (a video recording of which is freely available online). The poet – who was also at the time editor of *Modern Poetry in Translation* – opens by exploring what she calls the 'linguistic cosmology' of the Indonesian language itself ('a universe of speculative words, gestures, perceptions'), before delving into the etymology of the term 'amuk', found equally in the 'high decibels' of a child's tantrum and the 'primal scream' of the overworked grown-up.

It is, as we discover, a word with many intertwined and unsavoury histories: from the brutality perpetuated on indigenous lives and landscapes alike by colonialists, then capitalists; to the equally, if not more brutal crackdowns on the Indonesian left under Soeharto's dictatorship. These pasts are recounted in the numbered sections of a poetic sequence that shifts restlessly between voices; part song, part polysyllabic rant, part dutiful and sombre reflection:

> 'we will corporate-social-responsibility
> your revolutionary indigeneities
> and oil slick our way through
> the feel-good advertisement landscape'
>
> [iron and haze
> care not for how all waterways breathe
> with human blood as their inverse
> and keeper]
>   ('amuk i. waters')

The story Barokka saves for last is the transformation of "amuk" itself, a word 'changed by every element / wavy in the smoke / trembling under clear water / curved by the weight of stone'. Taking in this section a more didactic approach, she runs the reader – and stage audience – through the permutations by which the Indonesian "amuk" gave rise the English "amuck",

Re-created in book form, this text hovers with precision between affect and argument ...

an 'anglicisation steeped in bayonets'. How, she asks, could the anguished frenzy experienced by a colonised people have morphed into a 'pathologized', 'directionless', even 'homicidal' rage in the tongue of their colonisers? Barokka's answer is an oblique, but telling one:

> if someone enslaved your family
> including your relatives of animal, mineral,
> rivers worshipped and given names,
> would your efforts to free them
> by killing their captors
> be made into a feature film?
> ('amuk [infinity symbol]. waters')

Woven through these explorations of the past are hints of how the violences that define them continue to run amuck in the present. In one characteristic passage, Barokka reminds us – while looking up 'amuck' on her iPhone dictionary – that the device is 'created from poisonmines-shipping-poisoningfruit-workingtothebrink'. Thankfully, not all these interjections are equally on the nose. The book's briefer second section contains a series of more lyrical, standalone poems, many of which are titled as prayers ('prayer against the hunt', 'prayer as fistful of praise', etc.); since, as Barokka reimagines it, 'amuk is a prayer / is a word that prays / and is itself a unit of asking'. In one, alluding to the victims of the major Elephant and Castle fire of 2021, she writes of 'towers of people living out a dreamers' ending / of others' displacement', the 'brown solemnity' of those caught by forces beyond themselves. Up against history, there is little escape: nothing that 'could possibly cocoon from this: // your body and your family, / what prayers slam against' ('prayer for man in accident, elephant and castle').

Zaffar Kunial's *England's Green*, by now a much-lauded release, lends the perfect counterpoint to Mehri's and Barokka's books. Structurally, it is subtler in its efforts to stitch together either epic or argument from individual poems; two balanced sections – 'IN' and 'OUT' – lend their clean symmetry to the collection, while gesturing to triumphs and failures of the present-day Englishman's favoured battlefield: the green. Kunial also shares Barokka's fascination with etymological detail (an epigraph to the first section ponders the roots and relatives of the word 'in'), complementing this with a poet's close attention to the way words are worn out, worn down, and worn away in everyday life. His opening poem, for instance, dwells on the unwieldy sounds buried in its own title, 'Foxglove Country' ('... *Xgl* / a place with a locked beginning / then a snag, a *gl* / like the little Englands of my grief'); while almost too early into the collection, another poem plumbs the depth of the word 'Green' (flimsy green hat of a Christmas dinner, Tolkien's Wake Green Road, 'small grass roundabouts' synonymous with middle England ...), weaving these threads into a perfect, heartbreaking elegy for the poet's mother that forces the reader to put the book down for a moment. As any newcomer to England's green would know, enunciation is often everything, and wordplay a deadly serious business.

To break the English language down, with all of its foibles and inconsistencies, is to get under a country's skin, to 'come back to a place called Ings', as Kunial puts it – riffing off the name of a Yorkshire town that supplies one of many coordinates to the poet's grief throughout the book, as well as that most cruel of suffixes, conjuring the eternal present ('Ings'). It is also how Kunial is able to escape the locked insularity of most place-writing, and deliver a deeply personal landscape to the reader as he must have first encountered it, an 'unloosable knot' to be unpicked by learning its vowels and stresses ('Scarborough'). The book's second half replies in some ways to the first, most obviously in the case of 'O'' – a poem which is the chatty antithesis to its terse sibling from the earlier section, 'O'. In these poems, the longing for arrival is turned on its head, one never arrives but is always still arriving.

The various absences and obsessions of the collection come together at least in its final poem, 'The Wind in the Willows', a nod to a novel that has, perhaps more than any other, colonised bedtime reading around the world. Though the book stands 'unread' on his

To break the English language down, with all of its foibles and inconsistencies, is to get under a country's skin ...

childhood shelf, there's no escaping the 'garden / I vaguely remember, the way the leaves curtained / like shadows' – a mental image of England's green that forms so powerfully in the mind of every Anglophone student. It is also the poem in this book that points most directly to the act of writing poetry itself, a release of 'Old power locked. A gravity well / beyond mine', that the young Kunial felt when picking up a cricket bat for the first time. 'A gathered strength', he calls it; one that leaps off the green of the page, and into our hands.

About the Author

Theophilus Kwek has published four full-length collections of poetry, two of which were shortlisted for the Singapore Literature Prize. He is the 2023 winner of the Cikada Prize.

INDEX OF POETS AND POEMS

ANASTASIA TAYLOR-LIND
 All I have is a list of things 5
ANTHONY WILSON
 Aria on Hope 5
EMILY WILLS
 Mnemonic 6
 Famous 6
REBECCA CULLEN
 Oh Twenties 7
 Meanwhile they're demolishing the Broadmarsh Centre 7
GRAHAM MORT
 Triton 8
 Oyster Catcher Dawn 9
CHRISTINE WEBB
 Gift 9
RACHAEL BROWN
 Sunk Cost Fallacy 10
 Against all advice 11
MATTHEW PAUL
 Invigilator Slater 11
EMMA LARA JONES
 Outside the hospital 12
 God bless urban architects 12
SIMON ARMITAGE
 The Holy Land 13
MARY CHUCK
 A Flurry of Feathers 14
 Grandson visiting 14
 Letter to My Younger Self 15
JAY WHITTAKER
 An office pedestal unit completes its annual appraisal 15
PASCALE PETIT
 After visiting the Museum of Doors, Pézenas, 16
 The Frozen Zoo 17
 Stag Father 18
 Papa Guèpier 18
JAMES CARUTH
 Looking Back 19
 The Blackbird 19

ALICIA STUBBERSFIELD
 Resilience 20
 In the Supermarket 20
 Sister Mary Aquinas 21
IAN DUDLEY
 Stargazing in Atacama 21
ALEXANDRA CORRIN-TACHIBANA
 Haibun from East Lothian 22
 Life is Movement 23
TOM SASTRY
 Your revolution 24
 On my cousin's doorstep 24
 Rooftops and moon 25
 Oliver Cromwell 25
HELEN MORT
 Chicken Triptych 26
 Stroke Ward 27
MARIA TAYLOR
 Refresher at Faros 28
 Night Swimming at Faros 28
 Arrival into St. Pancras, London 29
JULIAN TURNER
 Thomas Traherne Has Hot Stones 29
PAUL STEPHENSON
 The Ladder 30
 The Young Officials 30
 First Weekend 31
 New Trainers 32
FIONA LARKIN
 Costume jewellery won't bring you back 32
RUTH SHARMAN
 Ghosts at Assos 33
 Beyond the weir 33
DUNCAN CHAMBERS
 Polonius 34
 Archduke Michael and his brothers 34
 My late wife's wedding dress 35
SARAH MNATZAGANIAN
 Dawn 35
DZIFA BENSON
 Broken Ghazal for Pink and Gravity 36
 Call Me Balthazar 36

LOU NEUBERGER
 The Poems of Yevgeny Yevtushenko 37
 Flightpath 37
CLAUDINE TOUTOUNGI
 The River River 38
 Cézanne Shuffle 39
JONATHAN EDWARDS
 Boss 39
BEN BRANSFIELD
 Theurgy 40
 July, Québec City 40
 Nantucket 41
 Teacher's Copy 41
ORLAGH O'FARRELL
 Auntie Pearl skirts the sea 42
 In the Middle of French 42
D A PRINCE
 Staying on for the credits 43
 '... in my average moments' 43
KATHRYN BEVIS
 How to Choose a Boy 44
 Simply Beautiful 44
JANE KITE
 Should I move the table first or the tins of paint? 45
 More tea? 45
KATE BASS
 Nest 46
 Agosto 46
SUE NORTON
 Return Journey 47
 Pomander Ball 47
MICHAEL SCHMIDT
 '80 around the corner now ...' 48
 Cocataté-pu-ché 49
CARRIE ETTER
 Seasonal 49
KATHY PIMLOTT
 The Passing Visit 50
 Coda: Tips on Avoiding Religion and Therapy 50

MARY FORD NEAL
About a Man 51
Palomino 51

PAUL HENRY
Sustained A 52
The Sleeping Sister 53
The Leaves Hold On 53

LAURA STRICKLAND
Self Portrait in Mixed Media 53

IAN MCMILLAN
Collecting Items for a
Memory-Based Piece 54
She Was Leafing Through Her Bible 54

PAM THOMPSON
My life caught up with me and said 55
Here's a map of the Miner's
Welfare Park 55
Traffic Lights 57

HELEN BOWELL
Nêspera 61

PRERANI KUMAR
Kali Lays Down Her Swords 62

EVA LEWIS
Broken yellow wallpaper / those days 62

LAURA POTTS
Night Song 63

RUTH YATES
Doncaster Pride 64

CALEB LEOW
Our Changelings 66
Hunger Pangs 67
Archipelago 67

FREYA BANTIFF
Working Debenhams' Late Shift 68
Yes 69
The Lie of the Land 69

IAN MCMILLAN
Tall in the Saddle 70
Coalpicking, Broomhill 71

DOREEN GURREY
Great Expectations 72
Paternal 73
Guest 73

LAURIE BOLGER
After Class 74
Mary and John's Ruby Wedding,
the Working Men's Club 75

MARY ALLEN
Skull 77
Finale 77

CLEMENTINE BURNLEY
Transit I 78
Transits II 78

MICHAEL GREAVY
Stowaway 79
Frank Worthington Relives His Wonder
Goal v Ipswich Town 79

LYDIA HARRIS
The Holm of Aikerness remembers women
said to be buried there 80
One of the seven has the gift of literacy 80

RAMONA HERDMAN
They offer me the moss cure 81
Brain fog, not me 81

LAUREN O'DONOVAN
Latrina Vox 82
The Steadfast Heart 83

ALI LEWIS
The Touch 88
The Best Thing About Falling 89
Putting the World Away 89

ALAN PAYNE
Fathers and Sons 91
Castaway 92
Mahogany Eve 92
Evening Glory 93
The Black Prince on the River Don 93

SHASH TREVETT
In Memory 95
These Were Their Names 95
Illegal Migration Bill
House of Commons, Session 2022-23
30 March 2023 96
When David Heard 97

JANE ROUTH
It's a mast year again 99
Idle talk, 99
Out of time 100
The dead never leave III 100
The verge, 101
An "Arctic maritime airmass impact" 101

Blind Criticism poem revealed: The poem 'Traffic Lights' from *Collected Poems in English* by Arun Kolatkar, is reprinted by kind permission of the publisher, Bloodaxe Books.

The North is a publication of The Poetry Business,
Campo House, 54 Campo Lane, Sheffield S1 2EG
www.poetrybusiness.co.uk

ISBN 978-1-914914-65-2

ISSN 0269-9885